From Handguns to Paintbrushes

Joseph "Jeff" de Leyer

A memoir is a book of memory, and memory has its own story to tell. This is a work of creative nonfiction. While the author claims all stories in this book are true, it reflects his recollections of experiences over time and his interpretation of conversations that took place. The author has done his best to tell a truthful story. The opinions expressed within this book are solely the author's personal opinions.

Jeffdeleyer.com
ISBN: -10: 0692908331
ISBN-13: 978-0692908334

DEDICATION

To my beautiful wife and love of my life,
you were the only one who loved me for
who I was, not what I was.

To my mother Harriet,
you did the best you could with a boy who was so out of
control.

In memory of "The Boss"
My Grandmother

CONTENTS

ACKNOWLEDGMENTS

Never in my wildest dreams would I have imagined "From Handguns to Paintbrushes" being published. This book was written during a very dark time in my life, and the purpose was to leave my story behind. I still can't believe a book I wrote in Black & White marble notebooks, while locked in a cell is published. Now when my wife is asked, "What does your husband do?" She can now replace "convicted felon" or the more realistic, "uh, uh, uh" with "published author." Speaking of my wife, I'd like to thank her for not only believing in me, but for being crazy enough to believe anyone besides her would be interested in reading my book. She had to deal with my temper tantrums and constant complaining about writing, when all I wanted to do was paint.

I would like to thank my amazing Critique Editor, The Real Writer, Christine Stewart. Although I've never met you, I feel like I know you from your pages and pages and more pages of notes. Thank you for tearing my book apart and giving me the direction to make the pages flow. I now write with your suggestion of "show don't tell."

I would also like to thank Bard College, especially Max Kenner and Daniel Karpowitz for seeing my potential. The professors at Bard challenged me and taught me to write in a way, my book will at least make a little bit of sense to the reader.

A special thank you to Prisontalk.com for offering support to not only my wife, but so many families who have loved ones incarcerated all over the world.

I would also like to give special thanks to those who have stood by my side. Patrick Minardi, Carl Klass, and the entire Dowling family. I am forever grateful.

And last but not least, everyone who read the book prior to publishing and said it was amazing. I know you guys probably just said

1

this to make my wife happy, but even if you were lying, it made me feel good too.

INTRODUCTION

My name is Joseph de Leyer, but everyone calls me Jeff and I am 40 years old. I am known in prison by my street handle; Dutch Blood and I was known in the streets as Jeff D, the New York Ecstasy Kingpin. In July of 1998 I was arrested and later convicted of a gang related murder over a drug deal gone wrong. In prison I was a high-ranking member of the United Blood Nation. I have been involved in gang wars, riots and countless nonsense. My education has been earned in classrooms located behind the walls of some of the most violent Maximum-Security Prisons in the state of New York. My skills as an artist have been perfected while locked in a cell where at times, the walls have felt as though they would crush me.

I hand wrote this story from a Maximum-Security prison cell where I am being held in Segregation because I can no longer get along with the men in the Gang I was once the leader of. I made up my mind to change my life for a new start and this put a target on my back. This isn't who I am anymore. I want to be able to look in the mirror and be proud of who I see. I ran the streets and took a man's life over money and I cannot change this. I am the one who messed up my life and this is a difficult reality to accept. People fear men like me, but I have learned fear is only for a minute but love is forever.

The sad reality is, I could have done anything with my life, yet I chose to chase a dream that only works out in the movies. There is no happy ending to a life of crime in real life. This book may seem like I am glorifying my life as a criminal, but this isn't the case. My story is about a man who had to finally grow up because my reality became a million pounds that I was forced to carry on my shoulders. Most of the people I have spoken of end up dead in one way or another. This is the story of how Art changed my life and how the love of my life, saved my life.

PROLOGUE

When I came to prison in 1998 I felt like a gangster and prison promotes the ideology; "the worse you are, the stronger you are." When I became a member of the Blood Nation I believed in the ideas of the cause. I was taught that Blood stood for Brotherly Love Overrides Oppression and Destruction. The five principles that are taught are Love, Loyalty, Respect, Trust and Honor. These are notable attributes. I was a rebel who needed a cause and I found it when I was chosen to be one of the first white Bloods.

I spent the first couple years of my sentence proving I was a loyal soldier and making my name known. I was white in a gang made up of Blacks and Latinos, so I did everything extra to prove I was worthy. I felt like I was the Vanguard of the people. I was passing on what I knew to the little homies. The moto was, each one teach one. The problem was, I only knew destruction.

I was reading books about great revolutionists and I felt like I was helping to make a change. I spent years of my sentence in solitary confinement or segregation, because there were repercussions to being a leader of an unauthorized organization in prison, but it was all part of the sacrifice.

Men I considered my brothers went home and were killed or came back to prison, but still I believed that being part of a gang was being part of something that gave some people the only structure they had ever known. I felt like it was my job to play my part. We were gang members, but I saw it as being no different than being part of the military, and we fought our fight.

The first few years of my sentence, I had many girls coming to see me and they all claimed to be my girlfriends. The type of women I chased were not the type of women a man marries. We may have had good times, but the ride would only last so long. New York state has conjugal visits and those 48 hour vacations are every prisoner's dream. However, to get these visits an inmate must one: stay out of trouble, two: be married.

I had a lot of trouble staying out of trouble because I loved the drama and I wasn't married because I believed that marriage should be a one-time thing. I would not marry a woman in prison, I wouldn't have as my wife in the streets. I had talked about it with a few girls, and quite a few girls were willing to marry me, but I wasn't in love. I didn't know love because I liked girls, I loved having sex with girls, but I never loved any of the girls I had been with, and I've been with many. I didn't love them, even though I told them I did.

A man cannot truly love a woman and cheat on her. If a man loves a woman, she will be enough for him. A man and woman should fit together to balance each other out. I didn't know about putting anyone's needs before my own. My whole life was about my own personal gratification and looking out for me. Even in prison, I was still juggling different women. I was selfish, and it always had to be about me.

It had been a long time since I did anything for the good of someone else. As a matter of fact, I had only done a handful of good things in my life and she was one of them.

ONE

GROWING PAINS

"Family is supposed to be our safe haven. Very often it is the place where we find our deepest heartache" -Iyanla Vanzant

I am the grandson of the Dutch immigrant Equestrian Champion Harry de Leyer. My father Joseph Henry de Leyer Sr. is the oldest of Harry's eight children. The pressure of trying to follow in my grandfather's footsteps, caused deep bouts of depression for my father. My father battled with personal highs and lows as well as an addiction with drugs and alcohol his entire life. My biological mother Claudia, I can remember meeting less than a handful of times.

My mother and father were high school sweethearts and were married very young. With two young children, the honeymoon phase didn't last very long. My mother and father were drinking and doing drugs and three years into their marriage, it was clear they had made a mistake. My father was considered by the court to be the more stable parent and was granted full custody of us. Although my father was awarded custody, he wasn't fit to tend to the needs of two small children.

When I was three years old, I was dropped on the doorstep of my father's sister Harriet. My sister Heather who was 18 months old, was also with me along with both of our worldly possessions. I came with less accessories than a cabbage patch kid. I had one pair of jeans, two shirts, a pair of sneakers and a rope which was used as a belt. However, my sister came with a chest full of dresses, shoes and other goodies.

Harriet was a newlywed to her first husband Terry, and as two young people trying to find their way in a tough world, they did not have the means to take on two children. Harriet and Terry were expecting their first child, so Terry told his wife they could only take one of the orphans. Harriet with a tough choice at hand, had to pick one of her brother's children. She didn't want to separate the pair, but she had to make a choice. She chose to take me because I needed more immediate care.

My sister was shipped a few blocks away to stay with another family member. My biological mother kidnapped my sister from the house she was staying at and took off. My father was dealing with legal problems in New York, so he fled the state and didn't make an issue over his daughter being taken by his ex-wife. I can only guess my biological mother cared more for my sister than she did me and this would explain why she left me behind. Later in life I would be told in a joking manner, "You showed up a hot mess, scrawny, dirty and in desperate need." I guess this is why Harriet chose me. Although she didn't give birth to me, Harriet is my only mother and throughout this book, I will address her as Mom.

Harriet and Terry raised me with their own daughter Charissa. Charissa was my sister and my biological sister was only a person I heard about in stories. My biological mother was a woman I didn't know, my mother was Harriet. Every once in a while, my father made guest appearances. Like most children who grow up with an absentee father, I had convoluted fantasies of what my father did and who he really was. My fantasies were better than the reality of things and this made his absence not hurt as much. Terry was good to me, but I knew he wasn't my father.

8

My father had 5 brothers and all but one were in New York. My mother used to travel out to East Hampton, Long Island on the weekends to teach horseback riding lessons at my Grandfather's farm. My uncles also worked on the farm. I was not a spoiled child, but I had things. I worked from the time I was old enough to be useful. In my family, everyone is part of the family business because it takes many people to run a horse farm and my grandfather was a firm believer in everyone getting involved. I learned a good work ethic that I would use later in life to climb the drug dealer ladder. Breaking and training horses makes a man real tough and I learned if a family worked together, they could make a business successful if everyone played their part. These lessons would also come in handy later in my life.

I learned about training horses from the Patron of the de Leyer clan. I also learned about being a man from my grandfather. My grandfather is a tough Dutchman and he has a stern firm hand. Grandpa started teaching me how to tend to the horses as soon as I was old enough to walk. He didn't care if I was four or five. If he felt I could do what he asked, I better at least try. If I was stupid enough to complain, a swift slap across the face would be enough motivation for me to try to do whatever he asked of me. This is just how it was. My Uncles who were all beer drinking brawlers knew better even as grown men to try the old man.

The horse business is a tough business and it takes tough men to work it. Some horses will kick and bite grown men, nevertheless a boy, but I was taught not to fear these 1200lb animals at a very early age. We didn't use a vet for simple things we could do ourselves, so Grandpa and my Uncles taught me what I would need to know.

Horses sometimes get boils on their necks that need to be cut so they can drain. In one of these lessons Grandpa had me in the stall with a horse who had a boil. Grandpa cleaned his swiss army knife and handed me the knife. I was only five years old and he told me I needed to stab the boil, so it could drain. I wanted to hold the knife, but I was scared to stab the horse. I remember hearing the horse's nervous breath and I felt like he was able to sense what we were about to do. I was scared with the knife in my hand, but I was also scared of not doing what my grandfather asked. I started to cry because I didn't know what else to do. Grandpa wasn't much for criers and I was trying to be strong, but I was a child. Grandpa said, "What are you shicken shit?" His accent didn't allow the "ch" sound. I didn't want to be "shicken shit" or chicken shit in my Grandfather's eyes because even at five, I wanted to be a strong Dutchman like my Uncles and Grandfather. I closed my eyes and swung the knife because I was more scared of my Grandfather than the horse itself. I missed the boil and hit the horse in the neck which caused him to flip out in the stall, but I was close enough to Grandpa, so I knew the horse couldn't get me. I may not have hit the target, but I proved I wasn't "shicken shit" and this was good enough for me.

My uncles were young and wild men and they made me tough and gave me a sense of family pride. This is a quality I still possess today. I learned about the role my family played in the fight against the Nazi's in World War II. When the German's invaded our country, my family took action against the Nazi party. The Nazi's had taken our horses off our brewery and helped themselves to whatever they wanted. My Great Grandfather and his children did their part to fight back. My grandfather would tell me stories how he and his brothers would blow up train tracks in an attempt to resist the Nazis. When the allies started parachuting in town, the Nazis would shoot them out of the sky as they were trying to land. My family would bury the fallen soldiers in the family cemetery we had on our property. One of my grandfather's sisters who could read and write English would write to the families and let them know where their loved ones were put to rest.

When the war was over, my Great Grandfather who had escaped to Europe, eventually came back to help rebuild our country. Grandpa had married my Grandmother and decided they would come to America. After the war, anyone wanting to come into America would need to be sponsored. One of the families of a fallen soldier buried on our property helped my Grandparents become Americans. My grandparents came to this country and created their own path. My grandparents were divorced all my life and even though my Grandpa moved on and remarried, my grandmother was never able to move on. She loved him until the day she died.

I did things kids did in the 80's in New York. I took Karate classes, played school sports, skateboarded, rode BMX bikes, surfed, snowboarded and rode horses on the weekends. The difference was, I came from a legacy and when I competed at horse shows, I was expected to win. Winning was good for the family business. I had been on a horse back before I could walk, doing Victory laps with Grandpa at Grandpre's.

When I was around 12 years old, I was still riding at times and when my family needed me to show, I did. In Harrisburg Virginia, there was a big horse show every year and I was sent down to help Grandpa. Grandpa had a stallion named Dutch Sparrow and we were an unstoppable team. I beat out Joe Fargis and Rodney Jenkins, two Olympian Equestrians. In the winner circle Grandpa gave me a smirk. He wasn't a very loving man, but his smirk was as good as it got, and it was enough to make me feel proud and worthy. I was always told when I didn't do something good enough, but I was never told when I did well because it was just expected of me.

Harriet and Terry were facing problems in their marriage and they eventually divorced. We ended up moving to Rocky Point, NY, and it was just me, my mother and sister Charissa. When we went to the Hampton's on the weekends, Charissa and I would hang out with the rich kids while my mom taught her lessons. We would tag along on their adventures or sometimes we went with Terry and did whatever he was getting involved in. Terry was a cool dude and he did a lot of cool things. Terry was a carpenter and came from a family of builders. He built me skateboard ramps, taught me about carpentry and even paid me to help on his jobs.

I was exposed to a lot of different people at a very early age. Equestrian riding is the sport of kings and it attracts people who are culturally rich. I learned how to sculpt from one of my mother's customers who was an artist. He and his wife didn't have any children of their own, and I guess this is why they enjoyed spending time with me and my sister. They would take us to their weekend house for the day, so we weren't stuck at the horse farm. He allowed my sister and I to twist the underwire to the poses for his sculptures. He also let us play with the clay. It was fun to get messy and play with the clay. I remember how I loved looking at his finished sculptures. I wasn't any good at sculpting, but I was having fun. I was also able to tag along to gallery shows and I found myself around all sorts of interesting people.

In my early years, I was introduced to the hip hop culture through the black kids who I had grown up with. Race is something that doesn't matter to kids and in my neighborhood, there was a huge Black family who lived on our block. I spent a lot of time with my friends. We would listen to Big Daddy Kane, De la Soul, the Fats Boys and Run DMC. I remember as a young kid how African Medallions were popular, and all my friends had them, so I got one. I came home with my Medallion on and my mother looked at it and said, "Do you know what that is?" I said, "It was African." She said, "Boy, you know you're white, right?" I said, "Yes" and that was that. My mother didn't have a racist bone in her body and neither would her kids.

I started writing graffiti to connect with the older kids who I looked up to. In the beginning, I wasn't very good, but I would tag up everything I touched. I would go out and steal cans of spray paint from any place I could get away with it. I became part of a Graffiti crew named Task Mob. We would get on our skateboards or BMX bikes with our Jansport book bags full of markers and spray paint and we were off, to leave our mark everywhere. Society called it vandalism, but we called it art. Graffiti gave me a way of being recognized as my own man. While I was tagging, I wasn't "Harry de Leyer's Grandson" I was just me.

Around this time my Grandfather had moved to a horse farm he bought in Virginia. My Uncle and his wife bought the farm from him in the Hamptons. I wasn't making as many appearances anymore because I was racing BMX bikes and the races were always held on the weekend. I was young, I just wanted to hang out with my friends. At this point, I was 10 years old and I was smoking weed and drinking 40's of malt liquor. To me, it was more fun to hang out in the hood with my friends then to be out in the Hampton's with the rich kids. The allure of the streets began to call me, and I was ready to answer.

My mom wasn't rich, she worked for the rich. We got to hang out with them and experience their lives because they would always include us. Mom was a single mother with two kids to feed and she only worked on the weekends. On the outside, we looked like we were doing well, but I was receiving free lunch at school. We weren't broke, but I needed to make my own money if I wanted anything extra. I had worked on the farm as a kid and I also worked for Terry from time to time, but I knew I didn't want to do manual labor. I already knew how this felt and it wasn't for me. My Uncles grew weed on the farm when they were young. They didn't grow a lot and it wasn't very good, but I knew where it was. When I would make my appearances, I was only 10 years old, but I already thought I was grown. No one could tell me anything. I would be smoking weed with my Uncles and drinking their cheap beer. My uncles eventually began to bribe me to work for weed. I'd train customers horses or show them in exchange for weed. My business moto at this time was, "Will work for drugs".

* * * * * *

On a farm, a young boy learns to drive farm equipment at a really young age and I could drive by the time I was nine. I had to drive the tractor to do the work around the farm. We had farm trucks that we used for different stuff and I learned to drive all of them. I was a young man, so I drove all this stuff as if they were go-karts. I could drive a stick or automatic, it didn't matter. One day I was at home hanging out with the older kids in my neighborhood and these guys came through and said, "Who knows how to drive? I raised my hand and they said, "Jump in the van." I wasn't afraid of anything, so I jumped into the van with the older kids and we were on our way. We arrived at a garage where there were a lot of cars in different stages of repair. The guys who had the shop were Greek and they would take the cars and ship them back to Greece. These men were seasoned criminals.

One of the men took one look at me and couldn't believe I knew how to drive. He wanted proof that I could drive so they put me behind the wheel of a 5.0 Mustang. The car is a stick, so I pushed the seat all the way forward and jumped behind the wheel. I turned the engine over, hit the gas and felt the rumble of the engine. This is enough to bring a cheesy grin to any young boy. I pushed the clutch in, put the car in first gear and dumped the clutch, smashed the gas and lit the tires up. I let this big boy toy red line and switch gears. I traveled around the block showing off until we made it back to where we started. Apparently, I did enough to prove I was worth teaching how to steal cars.

I finally found a job that was going to pay for my weed and beer. There would be no more smoking my Uncle's dirty home grown. The other kids and I were taught how to colonize cars and yank ignitions. These lessons were much more interesting than the bullshit they were teaching me at school and I enjoyed soaking in all this new knowledge. To me, this was information I could use. We were told we were each going to get $100 once we got the cars on the list. At this point in my life, this was big money. I could get rid of the Payless Olympia Sneakers I had on and get a pair of Adidas with the fat laces. No more four stripes for me. I had finally made it. Felony auto theft was not even a thought or worry to me. The fact that I had to steal three or four cars to earn this money never mattered to me and the truth as to how these old dudes were using my young dumb ass, didn't matter either.

The night I went out to steal my first car I was nervous yet excited. The Greeks picked us up in a van and I rode in the back with the other kids. The car I had to take was a black Nissan Maxima. They gave me a slim jim to open the door and a long screw driver to get the car started, dropped me off and left. I was nervous and a little shaky, but I was still able to catch the lock with the slim jim. I got in the driver's seat and pushed the seat all the way forward, so I would be able to reach the pedals. I titled the steering wheel down and stuck the screw driver in where the blinker was and broke the covering off. I now had a clear view and could locate the locking mechanism, I banged the flat head screw driver into the jaws of the lock until I got it to separate. With the car colonized, I started it up and was on my way back to the garage. When I arrived, the Greeks were clapping for me and told me how I had done a great job. I loved the praise and I felt like I was part of a team. I didn't realize I was being used, but the truth was, even if I did, I probably wouldn't have cared.

At this time in my life I wasn't even allowed outside after nine or ten o'clock unless I was going to a dance or something. This wasn't an every night gig, but when they would come looking for us, I would suddenly have a friend's house I was sleeping over and they were always my alibi for my mom. The problem with me knowing how to steal a car and drive was, I wouldn't only take cars when I was being paid to. If I needed a ride, my trusted tools were the keys. When the car is stolen, you become very reckless, hence the saying, "drive it like you stole it".

I was still going out and bombing with the boys. There is a sense of pride for a Graf artist when daylight breaks, and you see one of your pieces in all its glory. I never considered graffiti vandalism, I always thought it brought character to a neighborhood. Graf artists learn to be outlaws real fast because once you start making your rounds, the cops want to know who you are. There were always run ins with the cops and on this night the cops snatched me up. I wasn't caught in the act, but my backpack didn't have anything in it but spray paint, markers and caps. With every step I took, you could hear the clickety clack of the spray paint cans. The cops put me against the wall and they patted me down and searched my bag. They could have brought me into the station, but that meant paperwork and I was still under age, so it wasn't as though I was going to jail. It was the same with the cars. Under 16 years old, there wasn't much the police could do to a minor for these petty crimes. When the officers found all the spray paint, they took one of the cans out and made me turn around. The cop said, "Shut your eyes." I thought I was about to get a crack across my face, but then I heard the pressure of the aerosol being released as I felt the paint hit my face. I couldn't believe this was happening and I was pissed off. The officers painted my face and hands. They then threw my bag into the squad car and were gone. I looked like a smurf. Spray paint doesn't come off easily and I was going to have some explaining to do once my mom saw me.

The officers were smart, they worked smarter not harder. If they brought me down to the precinct, the only thing they could've really done was call my mom to come get me and present a case to PINS court that wasn't going to go anywhere. PINS stand for "Persons in Need of Supervision". A PINS petition is a written request asking the Family Court to get involved when other efforts to control a child have failed. The officers knew my mom was going to find out because I was covered in paint.

The walk home was the walk of shame because everyone who saw me had to point and laugh. I understood, I would have thought it was the funniest thing ever if it had happened to someone else. I got a beating for it once I explained what had happened. I spent two days trying to scrub the spray paint off my face and hands. Whoever stated the truth will set you free, has never had to tell the truth when they were dead wrong.

* * * * * *

I was on my way down the wrong path and my mother could sense it. Mom was my mother, father, nurturer and the person who was responsible for disciplining me. But at the end of the day, she was too much of a sweetheart and I really thought I was grown. My Grandpa was in Virginia, so I didn't have to worry about his wrath. My Uncles were instigators and I was their get high partner and helper when they needed to pull off their own capers. During this time, my father was doing very well. He married some rich girl whose father was some important doctor in Florida.

Dad was training race horses and running his own small farm, but his addiction was as strong as ever. My mother contacted my father and they discussed me coming down to Florida to spend the summer with him. By this point in my life, my mother was desperate and had hoped my father would be able to straighten me out. I was set to fly down to Florida and I was going to meet my biological sister Heather. I was told her stepfather did something bad to her and due to this, my father was going to get her back.

I was still racing BMX bikes, so my bike and I were packed up and loaded onto the plane. I was excited to see my father and meet my sister. Kids are lucky because they have the ability to forget that they have been abandoned in the hope they can have a future with the absentee parent. In my mind, I still held on to the fantasies I used to cope as a child. My father was trying to be a good Dad and I was happy for the effort.

When it was time to get my sister, we had to go to the Family Services building in Ocala, Florida. I was nervous and excited to meet my sister, but I didn't know what to expect. My sister was a stranger to me because the last time I saw her was on Harriet's doorstep. I was only 3 years old, so I don't even remember this, but I have been told the story many times.

My father and I were sitting in a waiting room when suddenly out of a side door, emerges a young girl and a very pretty short woman. My father stood up, so I stood up. It was clear that my sister was scared but we made our way to her. The short walk seemed to take forever. I noticed the woman standing next to my sister started to cry. I had no clue who she was, but she looked at me and said, "I am sorry." I didn't know what this woman was sorry for, I was confused and looked up at my father. She was walking towards me with tears running down her face and I was shocked and confused when she opened her arms and hugged me. I looked at my father and then back to the woman and said, "Who are you?" She said, "I am your mother." I said, "I don't know why you're crying, because I don't know you." as I pushed her away from me. I grabbed my sister's meager belongings and we started walking towards the exit. Claudia and my father spoke, but I didn't pay attention to what they were saying because I was looking at my sister for the first time.

When we got outside and loaded into my father's BMW, my sister and I watched as Claudia and my father continued to speak. When my father got into the car, he said, "Your mother wants to go bowling so we can spend time together. Jeff, is this all right with you?" My dad said, "Don't worry, I will come with you because I don't trust her." I agreed to go. My father started the car and we headed back to the house. My father's new wife made sure Heathers room was ready for her and when we arrived back at the house, we all hung out and just tried to make Heather feel comfortable. We asked Heather if she wanted to go bowling with us and Claudia, but Heather did not want to see her mother, so she decided to stay at the house with my father's wife. My dad was ok with this because this would give them some female bonding time.

My father told me it was time to go meet Claudia, so we hopped in the car and made a pit stop. My friend Andre was the son of my father's weed dealer. Apparently, my father needed to get high if he was going to spend the evening with his ex-wife. When we went to pick up the weed, I begged my father to allow Andre to come bowling with us and he agreed. When we got to the bowling alley, Andre and I stepped out of the car, so my father could smoke a joint. He could have smoked with me in the car, but I pretended I had no clue as to what he was about to do. Little did he know, I had been stealing his clips out of the ashtray the entire time I was in Florida.

Andre and I walked into the bowling alley, and once again, I saw this woman who claimed to be my mother. Deciding to play along, I allowed her to hug me. She said, "I love you." But I didn't believe her. If she loved me she would have never taken my sister and left me behind. While we were bowling, I really wanted to ask her why she had left me behind, but I was not brave enough, so I stayed silent for most of the night. Claudia said, "You have a brother." Yet I did not feel like any child of hers was a brother of mine. We all walked out to the parking lot and I allowed Claudia to hug me and kiss me on the cheek for the last time. In the spirit of getting along, I kissed her back on the cheek. When we got into the car Andre said to my father, "Joe, how did you let that one get away, she is beautiful." My father said, "That one right there, is crazier than all outdoors." This was the last time I ever saw Claudia.

Years later, one of my counselors in prison, Miss Scott, suggested we try and contact Claudia. Heather gave me the phone number and Miss Scott said she was going to call her. As an adult, I realized Claudia abandoning me had fucked me up. The next day, I was called to Miss Scotts office and as soon as I sat down Miss Scott said, "Baby I don't want you to worry about anything. I talked to Claudia and she doesn't want to speak to you, but there are people who love you." At that moment, I had already given up on Claudia. This attempt to reach out, was solely because I either needed answers or some form of closure. Her response may have shocked Miss Scott, but it didn't shock me. After all, this was the woman who abandoned me when I was 3 years old and never came back to get me. The only reason she saw me in Florida, was because I happened to be with my father when we picked up my sister. I was her first-born child and she didn't want anything to do with me then, so why should she want to have anything to do with me now?

That summer was one of the best summers of my life. I won every race I entered at Daytona's BMX park and picked up a sponsor from a company called Cycle Craft. I got to know my sister and being the bad influence, I was, I would steal weed from my Dad's stash and we would go to the barn and get high. Heather and I were being brother and sister for the first time. We wouldn't speak about my mother because she knew it would upset me. We spent that summer trying to build a relationship as if we were a happy family. My father took us to water parks, tubing and waterskiing. I guess he was trying to create childhood memories. At this point in my life, my father was doing well. When he was doing well, he tried to be a normal dad. Sadly, my father doing well didn't last past the summer.

The summer went by fast and before I knew it, it was time for me to go back to New York. My sister was settled in and we were able to live with each other for a while. Florida was cool, but I missed the mean streets of New York. I managed to leave my mark in Florida because I had gone on a few solo bombing missions. I had to bring a little New York Graf to the Sunshine State.

TWO

IN THE WIND

"Running away from your problems is a race you'll never win" -Kyle O'donnell

The sun and fun was over and it was back to the streets of New York. The Greeks I was stealing cars for had gotten busted that summer, so it was time for a new hustle. I had an idea and decided it was time for me to start my own business. I had picked up a BMX sponsor in Florida and although they didn't pay me, I was going to receive three bikes a year, racing pants, a jersey and a helmet with the logos. I sold my bike and took the money and bought weed. I had been smoking enough bud to know the size bags I needed to be able to get my work off. "Work" is a term drug dealers use for drugs.

I knew an older kid named Alex who used to ride at the practice track in the neighborhood. I had friends my own age, but I always gravitated towards the older kids. Alex didn't ride anymore, but he and his team were always around pushing weed. He had asked me before if I wanted to sell weed for him, but I didn't want to then. Now that I was ready, I would start to buy my own work. If I was going to work for someone, it was going to be for myself.

21

I had done things for the drug guys before like drop packages off or hide stuff when the cops came around. I did all of this for shorts (dollars, five dollars, little money, pocket change or weed), but I had watched the guys enough to know what to do. I was confident I could fake it to make it, so I was off to the races. I had my weed bagged up and all I needed to do was start making sales. The older guys who sold cocaine smoked blunts all day long, so I figured I could sell my little nickel bags of bud to them. They would make their sales and I'd make mine. All my friends smoked weed too so I knew I would be able to sell my product to them. I had finally found my new calling.

My business took off fast and I was making enough money to be hood rich for a young kid. Alex liked how I was hustling and he would pick me up and school me to the game. Everyone knew I was his little man. Alex only sold ounces and pounds. He had a nice new truck, a hot girlfriend and plenty of cash. He had everything I wanted. A lot of kids wanted to be professional athletes, doctors or cops. I however, wanted to be a drug dealer. The drug boys had it all in my neighborhood and what boy doesn't love his toys, guns, motorcycles and Barbie doll girlfriends?

The deeper I got into the streets the further away I slipped from my family. When I was around 13, my uncle Marty would come snatch me up and make me go to my Grandmother's house to help him train the horses he was trying to sell. I was conflicted. I enjoyed being with my uncle and doing what my family did, but I enjoyed running the streets more than the life that was predestined for me. During this time in my life, I cared more about my friends than the people who had my best interests at heart. I never had a strong father figure in my life, so I learned about being a man from everyone I was around, and I was mostly around criminals.

I recruited Matt one of my childhood friends to help with my business venture. Matt was unique in the fact that he was a white kid with red hair and freckles, yet he was Jamaican. His Jamaican heritage would help us later in life when we needed to make connections. I had

22

met Matt because I had dated his older sister Rachel when I was like 12 or 13. I had met Rachel at school and she was a tiny little red-haired girl. She gave me her number and I will never forget the first time I called their house. Jeremy Rachel's father, answered the phone and he had such a deep Jamaican accent. I thought I had the wrong number. When I asked to speak to Rachel, he said, "Hang on my youth". When Rachel got on the phone I said, "Who answered the phone?" She said, "My father." I said, "Is that your stepfather?". She said, "No, that's my father and we are Jamaican." As far as I knew, Jamaicans were black and most of them had dreadlocks. I said, "You're not Jamaican, you're white." But she said, "Nope, I'm really Jamaican." Rachel and I didn't work out as boyfriend and girlfriend, but even today I remain close with her family. Matt and Rachel remained a constant in my life. They were with me at my sentencing and with me throughout my entire prison bid.

Matt and I were both popular kids and we had a lot of mutual friends, yet we also had outside friends which gave us more area to cover with the business. Alex was supplying me with quality refer and when I rode around with him, I met the people he did business with. The guys who provided him with the pounds of weed owned a garage. They were much older. These were grown men. I had never done business with them before, but they saw me with Alex. Alex not only sold weed, he did a lot of drugs as well. He would disappear for days, in a hotel somewhere smoking crack. Alex's family finally forced him to check into rehab. Here I was, without a connect.

When Alex first came up missing, I did what I would have to do when I needed to re-up. Matt and I would go to Brooklyn and deal with the Jamaicans who were friends with Matt's father. The problem was, the weed was just regular green and the rude boys were always trying to get over on us. Plus, East New York Brooklyn was like the wild west back then, so I always brought the little .25 Caliber handgun I had gotten from one of the older crack dealers. I needed to figure something out because my entire business was surrounded around the fact that I always had the quality weed, not the same dirt weed that was

23

all over the hood. I had made up my mind, I was going to talk to the guys at the garage. The worst they could do was tell me to get lost. They knew I wasn't a cop, I wasn't even old enough for a learner's permit. I was smart enough to not steal a car to get to the shop because I didn't think they would appreciate the heat. I also didn't want to have anyone drive me because drug dealers are funny about people they don't know. After all, they really didn't know me but at least they had seen me with Alex. I threw all the money I had in my backpack. It wasn't a lot of money for a grown man, but it was all I had, and it was a lot of money for a 14-year-old kid. I got on my bike and was on my way to see if I could talk my way into a connect.

I finally arrived at the garage. The shop specialized in customizing four-wheel drive trucks. I had seen the main guy who Alex had always spoken to when I was with him, so I knew who I was looking for. When I spotted him, I was so nervous, but I needed this connect. When the old man spotted me, there was recognition in his eyes and this calmed my nerves a little. The old man stepped out of the garage into the back lot where I was standing, and he said, "Kid, where is Alex?" I said, "Alex is in rehab and I don't know when he is getting out." He said, "What are you doing here?" On the ride over I had worked out how I was going to go about this. I said, "I usually get my pounds from Alex but since he is gone I have been dry. I need work. I know many of Alex's customers and I can keep everything moving." I had ridden around with Alex enough to know the guys he dealt with. I didn't know if they would buy from me considering I was just a kid, but like I've said, sometimes you must fake it to make it. If I believed I could do it, maybe this guy would believe I could do it too. The old man listened to what I had to say. I was done talking and the old man was quiet for what seemed like forever and then he laid down the truth of the situation. He said, "Kid, I seen you before, but I don't know you. Alex and I had worked up a rapport and this takes time." But then his tone shifted, and he said, "I want to keep everything going and to do this, I have to move the weed. Everyone needs to play their part because this is the only way the business can carry on. How much weed do you think you can move?" I couldn't believe it, I was in there.

At this point in my life I was selling weed bag by bag. I sold ounces to Matt, but this was it. I had a triple beam scale I stole from the school science wing and I knew how to use it. A triple beam scale is the same type of scale you use to measure weight in science class and drug dealers us this to measure the weight of the drugs, so they can bag the drugs up by weight. I even had a beeper for my customers. Now I needed to figure out what to tell this man about my capability to move up the ladder. I needed to think quick and me freestyling had gotten me this far already, so I said, "I brought some money and as long as I have access to the pounds, I can make it happen. I don't need anything fronted to me until I know what I can handle." This was the truth of the matter. He said, "This isn't the way Alex and I work. With Alex, I gave him his load and he would do what he had to and then he would drop the money off." This made sense because then he wouldn't have to hold all the product, but I lived in the house with my mother and sister. My mom still did my laundry and cleaned my room. I ended up leaving the garage with two pounds of weed which cost me everything I had. But I saved $500 on each pound and I was ready to steal as many of my old connects customers as possible. Alex had taught me a lot about the drug game, but it was now my turn.

I started showing up at the houses I had been to with Alex and I let everyone know how I could now fill their orders. I even lowered the prices. I wanted to prove to my new connect that I could handle the weight, plus I needed to sway my new customers to only want to deal with me. I didn't know how Alex would feel about all of this, but at the time I didn't care. There isn't a business man alive who didn't step on a few feet to get where he was trying to go. Alex had been gone long enough and his customers were thirsty to do business. This mentality came to me very easily, I had grown up fighting my uncles to prove I wasn't a punk. The streets embraced guys who were too stupid to know better. I was fitting right in at this point. Alex had not told anyone he was checking into rehab, so it caught everyone by surprise. I wasn't the only one who was forced to sell the backyard basic weed to keep our business going.

I was moving through the pounds fast and I had to bring more of my friends on. When I was selling my nickel and dime bags, I used to hang out at this little park that had a handball court. I wanted to keep this going but I no longer had the time to sit in the park all day long. I decided to bring on some of my BMX crew. I was still riding and racing, but I spent more time riding from house to house selling drugs then I did on the practice track. But every Sunday me and the crew were at the BMX park racing. During this time, I wasn't going to school and mom was not happy. Mom believed my new girlfriend Rachael, (not Matt's sister) was a bad influence along with my friends. It's difficult for any mother to accept that their child is the one who was the bad influence and I was that kid. Mom was not stupid, she knew what was going on. She may not have known the full extent, but she knew I was fucking up.

Mom had a new boyfriend John and they had a daughter on the way. When I first met John, I instantly didn't like him, and my Uncles didn't really care for him either. John was just coming to live with us and he was already trying to implement rules in a household that was not his. He came to the door and wanted to play like he was the man of the house and my mother conceded to his rules. This bothered me. I was no longer a little boy and we had done just fine without him as far as I was concerned. I was the man of the house and suddenly I wasn't anymore. I felt like my mother chose this man over me and I was starting to feel like I didn't fit in their family photo. I didn't have a father figure and he had no desire to try and be a father figure to me. His approach was off, and I felt like I was an inconvenience to them. I couldn't adjust to this man calling the shots in my house, so someone was going to have to go. One day John decided to search my room and he found drugs. He was looking for a reason to get rid of me, so I eventually just stopped coming home.

I was staying from house to house. I would stay with Matt and his family or I would stay with the Dowling brothers and their mom. Momma D was a beautiful young mother who was gangster. Mamma D's house was on the corner basin, so the cops were unable to sneak up on the house because Dennis's room was glassed in on the porch. When the cops would come around they would either be looking for me or Mamma D's boyfriend. He had skipped out on parole and I was always on the run for one thing or another. But the neighborhood officers knew that if they got lucky, they could catch both of us at her house. We took our money from the streets, so warrants didn't bother either one of us one bit. But in this house, we had spent plenty of time hidden in the attic crawl space. There was no need to run because Mamma D was a beautiful woman who knew how to tell the cops what they needed to hear to get rid of them. In our neighborhood, the police were outsiders and we looked out for our own.

Alex had come back home, but I had already taken control of the neighborhood and he was out of the game. Alex was more of a hippy type dude, while me and my crew were more street and hood. If he had tried to take what I took from him there would have been problems. We didn't fight fair and all of us were either carrying guns or knives. The ideology projected in the rap music we were listening to was being manifested in our actions. We watched gangster movies and emulated our favorite characters and the streets were making us tough. We would defend our turf from anyone who was not part of our crew. The older guys from our neighborhood were afraid of us because the days of fighting on the block were over. If someone came around and was looking for problems, we would either jump them or shoot at them. I was now 15 years old and I thought I was grown. This was the problem with me. I always wanted to be older than I was. I started using drugs and drinking at 9, I was having sex by 11 and I bought my first gun at 12.

* * * * * *

Mom's best friend was a woman we called Aunt Kimmy. Aunt Kimmy used to come to the neighborhood and find me. She would take me to lunch and talk to me to see how I was doing. I knew she was my mom's spy, but I always went with Aunt Kimmy when she showed up. One day while I was on the block with the boys, Aunt Kimmy pulled up and said she wanted me to ride with her to go and pick up my uncle. Now when we were out on the block, we didn't keep money or drugs on us. Everything was stashed in case the cops rolled up. When Aunt Kimmy showed up, I jumped in the car with nothing but a Das EFX tape in my pocket. Aunt Kimmy told me we were going to LaGuardia airport to eat lunch and pick up my Uncle who was supposed to be flying in from my Grandfather's new farm in Virginia.

When we arrived at the airports food court, we sat down and started eating. The food court was on the second floor. We were eating and I'm not thinking that there is anything out of the ordinary until Aunt Kimmy starts crying. I said, "What's wrong Aunt Kimmy? Why are you crying?" She said, "I'm sorry, this is for the best." At first it didn't register how I had been set up, but as soon as I figured out something was wrong, I saw the cops coming up the stairs with a woman in civilian clothing. I was looking for an exit, but I was caught. I looked at Aunt Kimmy and she was still crying and mumbling about this being for my own good. I felt so betrayed.

The woman comes straight to me and introduces herself as officer Hammer of the Family Court Services. This was the first time I had met her, but it would not be the last. Officer Hammer said, "You have a choice. We can take you into custody, or you can get on a plane and go live with your Grandfather in Virginia." For a kid under the age of 16 years old in NY, it is against the law to skip school and not live in a home with a legal guardian. I was guilty of both things as well as a laundry list of other crimes. I didn't want to go to Virginia, but I didn't want to go to kiddy jail either, so I chose the lesser of the two evils and got on the plane. I was off to see Grandpa and his second wife Grandma Joanie. I spent the entire plane ride plotting my escape. I wasn't excited to see my Grandfather because I knew he was going to work me like a dog. All I wanted to do was go back to the life I was creating for myself.

Grandpa's property was in Dike Virginia and Dike was in the middle of nowhere. Grandpa's horse farm was a 66-acre spread that had at least one hundred horses on the property and everything you could imagine for training equestrian champions. On a farm this size there is always a ton of work, plus all the horses need to be ridden and trained. I was free labor, and my Grandfather had already broken me in as a child, so I knew he was going to put me to work.

As soon as I walked off the plane I saw Grandpa and Grandma Joanie waiting for me. Grandpa was not a happy type of man and he was also a man of very few words, but in his own way, I knew he was happy to see me. I think Grandpa believed he could straighten me out. In his eyes, I was the hope for the next de Leyer equestrian champion. I grew up on horses, and some people have the touch. My family has the touch.

The next day I was woken up at 5:00am by Grandpa. 5:00am is when I was used to going to sleep, but at Grandpas, this was the beginning of a day of hard labor. I came down the stairs, and Grandma Joanie had already prepared a breakfast of eggs, bacon and toast made from fresh bread she baked daily. After eating breakfast, Grandpa and I made our way up to the barn.

The first thing that needed to be done was feed and water the horses. While Grandpa fed them, I filled their water buckets. From there, it was time to turn the horses out into their paddocks. With the horses placed where they needed to be, it was time to muck the stalls. I jumped on the tractor attached to the manure spreader and pulled it into the middle of the barn. Mucking stalls is strenuous back breaking work. I had not been used to this kind of work in quite some time. The callouses needed to sling a pitchfork, had gone away a long time ago. With all the stalls mucked out, it was time to start the training cycle of the horses. For the rest of the morning, I got off one horse and got on the next until it was time for lunch. At lunch time, we headed back to the house to eat and I was in pain. My legs were sore, my back hurt, my hands were raw, and I was ready to go. I needed to get back to my life of comfort I had become accustomed to.

When we were done eating lunch, we jumped in Grandpas truck to go speak to his neighbor about purchasing hay. Grandpas nearest neighbor lived at least a half a mile away. Grandpas neighbor was a character straight out of a hillbilly movie. He was a huge man in overalls with a big wad of chewing tobacco sticking out from his missing teeth. My Grandfather and the hillbilly conducted business and once they were finished, Grandpa told me to get out of the truck and follow him and his hillbilly friend.

A short way into the woods, I saw a contraption that I would later find out was a still to produce moonshine. Spending most of my life in the civilized world, I really didn't believe that moonshining still existed, yet here I was standing in front of proof. The hillbilly asked my Grandfather, "Is the boy old enough to drink?" My Grandfather, in his thick Dutch accent said, "The boy has already been to jail!" The hillbilly poured a generous amount of clear liquor into a glass jar for me and he poured himself twice as much. Feeling like I was grown, I attempted to take a deep swig and as soon as the moonshine hit the back of my throat, my mouth and throat were on fire. It tasted like I had just swallowed a mouth full of starter fluid. I began to sweat profusely and attempted to hand back the glass jar. Grandpa was laughing because he seemed to find this quite amusing. Grandpa said, "You must finish what is in the glass." With much dismay, wanting to be a man, I did what I was told. I was drunk as a skunk.

I stumbled my way back to the truck, so we could go back to barn. Grandpa, thinking he was funny, decided that he would put me on his problemed horses. When I was given a leg up into the saddle, I almost fell off the other side. With my feet underneath me finally, I eventually managed to get my feet in the stirrups. I did well for the first couple of minutes, but the minute the horse decided he was going to play his games, the moonshine did not work out well for me. I was tossed off the horse to Grandpas amusement. Grandpa was not a laughing type of man, yet he found all of this quite hysterical. As far as I can remember, this had been the only time I had seen him naturally laugh the way that he did.

My money, drugs, clothes and life were in New York. I went from chasing "easy money" to working like a dog for no money. I continued plotting my escape from the moment I arrived. I wasn't stupid. I knew if I didn't get back soon enough, I would lose everything because someone would eventually do to me as I did to Alex. In the drug game, one person falls off and the next gets promoted. One of my Grandfather's neighbor's son's jeep was parked in the barn while the son was away at school. Grandpa had gotten a couple of days of work out of me, but getting up at 5am and working and riding until sundown was not going to work for me. I had stolen plenty of cars already and one more would be added to the list. I knew how to get to the main highway from the farm and I would find my way home.

I worked all day with Grandpa and knew he went to bed around 8:30pm. I waited until Grandpa and Grandma Joanie fell asleep. I've never been a coffee drinker, but I was tired, and I had a long drive ahead of me. I brewed a pot of coffee, poured it into the thermos, made a sandwich and took the 6 pack of Heineken that were in the fridge. I trekked up to the barn and jumped into the Jeep, threw my Das EFX tape in the tape deck and was on my way.

When I was on the road, I cracked a beer and was ready to get back to my life. I had $22 and two cans of gas I had siphoned out of the tractor and a hose to siphon more gas on the road. I was on the Virginia Highway heading towards Washington DC and I was feeling good. All of a sudden, I heard sirens and saw flashing lights in the rearview mirror. There is nothing in the world that will scare the shit out of you more than driving a stolen car and seeing those lights. I shifted lanes and watched as the flashing lights passed me. It ended up not being a cop car, but an ambulance. My heart was beating out of my chest.

I stopped drinking beer and decided to get focused and eventually made it into DC. I had been there as a child with my mother and sister but now I was trying to make it home. I passed the White House and turned off the block and it was clear the guys on the street were selling drugs. I jumped out of the Jeep, bought a nickel bag of weed which was stupid because I didn't have enough money already, but my life had not been filled with good choices at this point anyway. I received directions from a guy on the corner and was on my way. I sparked up a joint, cracked another beer and drove off.

When I got into Delaware, I saw a toll booth, but no one was in it. I noticed the other cars stopped to take something, but I just blew through the booth. When I got to the toll booth at the end of the state, they asked me for my ticket. I didn't have one because I didn't know I was supposed to take one. I explained that I didn't have one and I was told I could pay $150. I explained how I didn't have this much money on me. I was then told I could give them my driver's license and they would send me the fine. I was in trouble, but God protects idiots. I turned the Jeep around and drove all the way back to get the ticket. Once I got the ticket, I noticed my gas was low. Even though gas was cheap back then, I needed the little bit of money I had for tolls. I pulled off the highway into the parking lot of a Motel and I emptied the two gas cans I had in the jeep. I used a screwdriver to pop a cars gas cap, fed the hose down into the tank and got a mouthful of gas before I got a flow, refilled the cans and put the gas in the jeep. I was back in business.

I was finally back on the highway and headed back to New York. I took I-95 north and followed the signs. By this time, I was tired as hell. I had worked all day and it was late. The beer and the weed didn't help either. I was fighting to keep my eyes open, but fatigue was winning, and I fell asleep at the wheel. I don't know how long I was out, but it couldn't have been very long. I awoke to the sound of a siren behind me. I snapped out of my slumber as the cop car passed me cursing out the window as he rushed to whatever emergency he had been called to. Luck was on my side once again. If not for luck and God's protections of idiots, I wouldn't be alive at 40 to tell you this story. When I got to the point where I'm about to enter New York, I no longer had any money left for tolls, no gas and it was day break, so I couldn't try to pull one last move. I pulled off the highway at the gas station and I made a deal. For a full tank of gas and $20, I would sell them the Alpine Benzy box car stereo. With the deal done, I was back in New York.

I pulled up at the park in my neighborhood and the boys were out there. Matt was at school, but Chris was there, and I had clothes at his mother's house. We threw his bike in the jeep and headed to his house. I filled Chris in on what happened and how I got back. After I was clean and changed I beeped my girlfriend Rachael. She was at school, so we had to wait for her to call back between classes. She called back, and I got yelled at for not calling while I was gone. I didn't call anyone while I was gone. I needed to get to Rachael because my money was stashed at her parent's house. I still had to meet up with the boys and see how much weed was left. I was back, and I needed to tend to my business. No one knew what had happened to me because I didn't call anyone from Virginia. I knew I wasn't going to be there long and I didn't want anyone to get any ideas about taking off with my money or weed. It was better to keep them wondering. I wasn't gone long enough for everyone to dry up.

The school Rachael and Matt went to had alarms on the doors. I told them I was in a white Jeep Wrangler and when they saw the car, to hit the doors and come on. I pulled up in front of the school and as soon as I came to a stop, the side door opened and out ran Matt and Rachael. Rachael was a tiny thing, but she was moving. As they were getting into the Jeep, security was responding to the alarm, but they were too late. We were loaded in and I was laying rubber. I could have just taken off, but I was a young punk who thought he was badass. I jumped the curb onto the grass area of the school where the flagpole was, and I ripped the grass up with a pedal to the metal donut. Matt's parents were at work, so we decided to head back to his house. I needed to go over the numbers of the business, plus I wanted to get some pussy. I was young and horny, and it had been a couple of days. We hung out at Matt's house, made food, smoked bud, played Sega and I made phone calls. I needed to talk to the old man and make sure he was ready to see me. I wasn't going to mention how the cops were going to be looking for me, even more than usual. The cops were always looking for me. It was my job to avoid them and it was their job to try and catch me.

I was home, and it was back to business as usual. We had switched the plates on the Jeep and I was driving the thing around as if it was mine. Two weeks had passed since I left Virginia. I pulled up across from the Bodega in my neighborhood and jumped out to pick up a couple of 40's of malt liquor. I left Matt, Rachael and Chris in the Jeep. When I came out of the Bodega, my boy Brian who lived around the corner grabbed my arm and was leading me down the block. I looked over my shoulder and saw how the cops had the jeep surrounded. I made it around the corner before they arrested Chris. Chris had told the cops he had stolen the Jeep. I had loyal friends and in my neighborhood, no one trusted the cops.

The only problem was, the owner of the Jeep wasn't pressing charges. They knew I stole the Jeep and the cops were trying to catch me and send me back to Virginia. Chris tried to take a bullet for me and this made the cops even more pissed off because they knew they wouldn't have the cooperation they wanted. We were wild kids, but we protected our neighborhood from outsiders. We would fight amongst each other, but let someone from another neighborhood try anything and they would be fighting all of us. They eventually released Chris from jail. He wasn't old enough for them to do anything, plus, they knew he didn't steal the Jeep. I couldn't stay at his house anymore though because the cops would look for me there.

In my neighborhood, we had a detective we called "Timmy the Terminator". Timmy was a blue and white beat cop and he became a narcotics detective. He knew all of us because he had watched us grow up. The problem with the Terminator was, you never knew what you were going to get. Some days he would pull up on the block and ask us if we were holding it down and pull off, but other days he and his partner would jump out and search us and try to lock us up. I have been fast my entire life and I always run or try to run every time the cops tried to snatch me. I have always made the cops work for theirs. I like to fight but with the cops my first option is always flight.

The problem for me and my crew was, the Terminator knew all our habits. We weren't seasoned criminals yet and a creature of habit is easy for a hunter to trap. It technically wasn't Timmy's job to catch me for what I was wanted for. My legal issues were for running away, not going to school and whatever else may have been in my family court file. But officer Hammer's crew wasn't going to get it done. They didn't know the neighborhood and where I was likely to be. The problem was, the Terminator did.

Rachael's parents' house was on the corner. Rachael's father owned several of the homes on the block and their backyard wrapped around the back of one of the rental properties. On several occasions, the cops had tried to snatch me at Rachael's house and I would cut through the back to get away.

We weren't allowed to smoke in Rachael's house, so we would sit on the stoop and smoke. Rachael and I walked outside to grab a quick smoke and I caught the Buick Regal out of the corner of my eye. The Buick was one of Timmy's undercover cars. I wasted no time and I was off. I headed towards the backyard, so I could come out on the next block and I was stopped dead in my tracks by another cop with his pistol drawn. I was still looking for somewhere to go when I heard Timmy say, "run and I'll put a bullet in your back". Looking back on the situation, I don't know if he would have done it, but I know I believed him back them. Rachael watched me get handcuffed and placed in the car.

I was brought to the precinct and placed in a cell by myself. A couple of hours later, Officer Hammer shows up and said, "I tried to cut you a break, but you messed it up." I wasn't really paying her attention because I knew I had fucked up. I had fucked up because I had allowed myself to be caught, not because I had stolen the Jeep and come home. I wouldn't be getting picked up by mom.

I ended up getting transferred to a place called Montfort House. Montfort House was a holding place for kids before they had to see the family court judge who would then decide what to do with them. There were guards, but it was basically a house with a small school next to it. We didn't wear uniforms, we wore our own clothes and there were boys and girls at the house. It wasn't that bad, but I was plotting my escape the minute I arrived and told all the other kids I was going to get out of there. The guards and counselors were nice enough, but I had rabbit in my blood and things to do.

At night time, they took our sneakers and the rooms had alarms on the windows. This place had only one gate around the property though, so I knew it was going to be a piece of cake. The hospital was across the street and the train station was up the block. I didn't have any money on me, but this wasn't going to stop me. The next day I went outside with one of the girls who was in the house. We were shooting the ball around and the guard was sitting under a tree reading his newspaper. I whispered to the girl, "throw the ball over my head and into the woods." I backed up and she did as I asked. I went into the woods, threw the ball back to her and tore ass to the fence. I was up and over it before the guard even realized what was happening.

I was free once again. I ran as fast as I could to the train station. I didn't have time to wait for a train so when I finally caught my breath, I got into a cab. I gave the cabby the address to my neighborhood and we were off. I didn't have any money, but I had jumped plenty of cabs before. I would wait until we got into my neighborhood and then I would jump out and run. I did just that. Going back to my neighborhood wasn't really the smartest idea, but where else would I go?

Rachael told everyone what happened so everyone was shocked when I popped up on the block. I had to be careful though because it was daytime. For the next couple of days, I would spend the days at one of the boy's houses, and only come out at night. Vampire life was alright with me. The problem was, everyone else was still going to school so they couldn't hang out with me all night long. I had only made it a couple of weeks before I was caught again.

I went into the same Bodega I did the day Chris tried to take the Jeep charge for me and when I came out with my beer the cops had boxed me in. Everyone was across the street and they watched me get dragged off once again. I ended up going through the same routine with officer Hammer except this time, she was even more pissed. They ended up bringing me right back to the place I had just run from. When I went back some of the same kids were still there. I was told I had lost my privilege to go outside and play at recreation time. This time the staff kept a closer eye on me because they knew I was a runner and I would hate to disappoint them. I wasn't going to stick around this time either.

To give the guards a little bit of credit, the second go around they almost got me to court. It may have taken me a couple more days, but once the weekend rolled around we had a field trip to the Brooklyn Aquarium. The staff was trying to keep their eyes on me, but one of the kids in the house was a jouster, so they had to make sure to keep an eye on him. A jouster is a pick pocket. The jouster gave me some money and when they tried to load us into the van to leave, I took off. I always wondered why the other kids didn't try to run like I did. They didn't even try to chase me, and I was on my way back to my neighborhood.

I had been back a couple of weeks and Aunt Kimmy pulled up on the block once again. She had tricked me once before, but I loved her, and I knew she loved me. Aunt Kimmy told me my family wanted me to go live with my Grandma on the horse farm in Saint James. They made some sort of deal with the family court judge and Officer Hammer.

I spent the summer hanging out with my boys, but when September came it was off to Grandma's house. Her house was beautiful. I only knew a few kids from that area, but I had a cousin who would be in school with me. My old neighborhood was lower to middle class, but Grandma's neighborhood was a very wealthy neighborhood. Hold onto your wallets rich kids, the candy man is coming to town.

THREE

TO GRANDMOTHER'S HOUSE I GO

"I've got some issues that nobody can see and all of these emotions are pouring out of me" -Kid Cudi

It was 1991 when I went to live with my Grandmother. Grandma's house was always a safe haven for all de Leyers. I knew it wasn't going to be so bad because I loved and respected my Grandmother. In my eyes, my Grandmother was everything a woman should be. She was strong and even though she stood at only 5'3", she could control men and boys alike. My grandparents were divorced for many years, but my grandmother had always been in love with my Grandfather. After she had a little too much wine one Christmas, I was informed my Grandfather was the only man she had ever known.

I didn't look like the other kids I was about to be going to school with. I had a long blonde surfer/skater haircut, my pants were at least two sizes too big and I had a 30" gold chain with a Jesus head medallion on it. I also wore a black and white eight ball jacket that was in the news because guys were getting killed for it in the city. It was obvious on my first day of school that the kids had never seen a white kid who looked like me. I walked into my new school and everyone stopped and looked at the me. A girl who used to take riding lessons with my Uncle saw me and gave me directions to my homeroom. As I traveled through the school on my first day everyone was staring at me. I didn't care because I was only going to school to make my mom happy and to keep the cops from locking me up. My mother loved me, she just didn't know what to do with me at this point. Even though I was acting wild in the streets, I respected my mother and Grandmother because they were the only ones who truly loved me. The problem was, I was so adamant about doing things my way and I refused to listen to reason.

I had a plan. I would go to school then get back to my neighborhood to take care of business and then go back to Grandma's house at night. I wasn't trying to make friends because I already had my crew in my neighborhood. I had an art class and I was sitting in the classroom working on an outline of a character and the other kids were watching. One of the girls came over to me and started speaking to me and asking me questions. She was cute, she was a cheerleader. As we were leaving the classroom the cheerleaders boyfriend was waiting for her with a couple of his friends. I got a few dirty looks that I laughed off and I went about my day.

I left school and went back to my neighborhood. The next day I went to school, I ran into my cousin Shane. I went to my classes and when I went to art class, I talked to the cheerleader girl again. She was cute and like I said, I liked to flirt. When class let out I was talking to her and her boyfriend didn't like it. We had a few words. I wasn't the type of guy to take shit from anyone, especially a spoiled rich kid. The basketball star was feeling himself because he had his little crew with him. I was invited to fight after school at the "rock". I was laughing and told him I would be there.

The news flew around the school how the new kid was going to fight the basketball star. I wasn't worried about the fight. In my old school, you didn't get invited to fight, the shit just popped off. My cousin Shane found me and he was all nervous. Shane was a big kid and a terror on the football field, but he was never a fighter. I was told how to get to the "rock" and when I got there it looked like half of the school was there. There was a huge rock and a clearing that was behind where the handball court was. The area was hidden but there were so many kids there I didn't know how security didn't figure out something was going on. But the buses were coming, so I guess they were all in front of the school.

When I walked up, Mr. Basketball was putting on his tough boy act. I don't know what he thought but I walked up to him and started throwing punches. I've never seen a reason to talk before I fight anyone. If it's time to throw down, let's get to it. The kid was bigger than me, but size doesn't matter if you can't fight. I was putting the blows on this kid but he was too tall to fight inside so he tried to wrestle. When I went to school in my old neighborhood, I was on the wrestling team and I had made it to the counties in 7th and 8th grade. I was on top of this kid in seconds and was smashing his head against the ground. I didn't think it would be long before Mr. Basketball would pass out when suddenly, I'm hit from the back. I swing an elbow and I connect with the person who was trying to jump in. The only problem was, it was the cheerleader and before I knew it, fists are coming from every angle. I had been jumped plenty of times so I knew what to do. I just swung on any target I locked in on. As I'm fighting for my life, someone handed me a book bag with a rock in it. Once I started swinging the bag, my would-be attackers backed up and thought twice about coming within range. Now that the fight was over, it was time for me to boogie and catch my bus. I had a couple of bumps and scratches but it wasn't a big deal.

The next day the fight was the talk of the school. The kid who handed me the bag with the rock in it was an Irish skater named Tom and we linked up. I thanked him and asked if he wanted to skip class. This was his school so I followed his lead and we cut out a side door and walked towards a trail that led to a clearing in the woods. There were about twelve kids hanging out and smoking weed. I always had weed on me because it was my business and during this time I smoked like a mad man. These kids were smoking joints and bowls. I smoked blunts and I always had a box of White Owls on me. White Owls are cigars and the leaf of the blunt is used to roll up weed. I cracked the blunt and broke out my bag of weed. When the kids saw my bag, they asked, "Do you sell weed?" I said, "Yes" and they broke out cash. I hadn't thought about opening shop out there because my business was in my neighborhood, but these kids held cash. I served them and collected their money. I made sure to give out my beeper number and promised to have weed every day.

Tom told me he sold acid. He collected the money and went to Stony Brook College and saw his connect. This is where he picked up the acid and he made a dollar on each hit he sold. My drug business was much bigger than Tom's, but the fact that Tom was hustling meant he knew the kids who got high. This was a big school and these kids seemed to have money. For god sakes, there were BMW's and Benz's in the student parking lot. In my neighborhood, the only people rolling like that were the drug dealers. I had been around people with a lot of money in the horse world, but this was my first shot to get some of their money for myself. Tom introduced me to all his friends and people who I could do business with. I wasn't going back to my old neighborhood as much because I was making money in this new area and these kids had much better parties. You must understand, in the upper-class areas of Long Island, the cops are only writing speeding tickets, not looking for guns and drugs. Drugs were all around, but no blood was being shed so the community didn't care because it wasn't noticeable.

The kids I hung out with were the skater kids. I had learned to skateboard and surf as a kid and I got back into it with my new friends. These kids had half pipe ramps in their yards and cars to load up with surfboards to go to the beach. It was a good life; the girls were cute and I was sleeping with as many of them as I could. I've always been good with the girls and everyone knows little rich girls love to fuck the bad boys. During this time, I had turned my blonde hair into dreadlocks. I was different and they had never seen a white boy who had swag like mine. I've always did my own thing and my style was becoming ghetto star/skater and I had money to stay in what was fresh. I would shop in the City every week.

I was hanging out in the Commons one day and Tom introduced me to a group of girls. One of the girls was a cute brown-haired, brown-eyed girl named Joy. She had her pinch-rolled pants on and a pull over and when I looked at her she gave me the cutest smile in the world. She was a Freshman and only 14 years old. I was only a year older than her, but the life I lived was something she had never experienced. Joy and I clicked right away and we became very close. I could talk to her about anything. When I was with Joy, I felt like a normal teenage boy and we did normal teenage things. We hung out at Grandma's and she would come with me when the boys and I would go surfing. She wasn't like the other girls I was used to dealing with. Joy had this innocence about her and her innocence caused me to be very overprotective of her. By this point in my life, I was smoking weed and doing drugs every single day. Joy wasn't using drugs and I made certain she would stay that way. She did smoke cigarettes, but to be honest, I don't even think by this point she knew how to inhale.

Every Friday and Saturday night there would be at least a hundred kids hanging out in a mile-long stretch of Smithtown, known to the kids as "uptown". There would be groups of kids just hanging out, getting drunk, high and this was a gold mine. I would get a ride to the strip and once I was there I would get on my skateboard and make my rounds. One of my stops was always the pool hall. I would check to see if Joy was there and I would make sure she was ok and make sure no one was bothering her. Once I knew she was good, I would push off and finish my rounds.

I was selling my work and I started bringing coke out there because I had met a few older dudes who liked to sniff. The cops left everyone alone unless a fight or something broke out. Even then, no one went to jail. I met these people through Tom and we were usually together and those kids loved LSD. Toms connect was a dude we called Andy's

Candy's. He was a skater who went to Stony Brook College. On the weekend, he would pull up in his tricked-out Mazda and sit in the car listening to Techno music. Tom and I would run around and handle the business of moving the tabs of acid. Andy knew who I was because I had taken trips to the college with Tom to pick up his work. I was also easy to spot because I didn't look like the other kids. It was 1991 and a white kid with dreadlocks was easy enough to pick out of the crowd.

Tom had not shown up for some reason and when I was making my rounds, I noticed Andy's car. I skated up to him and told him I didn't know where Tom was, but everyone was looking for Acid. I told him to give me the work and I would take care of it. I knocked off everything I could and I went back to Andy's car. He was kicking it with a girl but kicked her out of the car so we could do the math. I had a nice take on me because I did my work plus I took care of Tom's customers. Andy saw I was a real hustler. Tom worked for Andy but he worked for pocket money and a free high. I was a different kind of money kid. Andy asked me if I wanted to hang out so I jumped in the car and we headed to the College.

When we pulled into the Campus parking lot, Andy asked me if I wanted to drop a hit and go skating. I had taken acid before and was starting to eat more of it with my new friends. We took the hits and went up to Andy's dorm room. Andy's dorm was hooked up nice. We put up the money we had and the rest of the drugs, rolled a blunt, grabbed our skateboards and we were off. Our adventure was fueled by a mind laced with grade A LSD. I really don't know how we didn't break our necks skating. When we were done skating we went back to his dorm room. It was cool because he didn't have a roommate and we just chilled playing video games until we finally fell out.

I didn't have any place to be because I was a drug dealer and when you're a drug dealer you make your own hours. I had been to the campus a bunch of times, but I had never really explored the school grounds. Since Andy was a student there, he showed me around. We talked about everything and I told him about my old neighborhood and how I ended up at Grandma's. I ended up talking Andy into selling me two sheets of acid. (one sheet is one hundred hits) It took some fast talking because he had a good thing going so I bluffed and told Andy I could get LSD from my old hood and do my thing with Tom. I could have tried to go into Central Park and tried to find the hippies, but half of the time you would get beat. I needed Andy's connect because I saw the money that was in LSD.

I already had the plan. I would keep Tom running the hits, but I would be the one to give him his work and I'd make it easy because instead of collecting the money and coming through the next day at school, we would have what they wanted, when they wanted. I wanted everything to come through me so I could make as much money as possible. I was only fifteen years old, but I was driven. All my life I have worked hard to make things happen. The only problem was, I've always directed my energy in the wrong direction. I was never satisfied with what I had, I always wanted more. This is the problem with greed.

I have always been able to get the guys to work with me but I didn't want to hand to hand the work because I had a need to be the boss. I wanted money and power. What I did was start flows and then hand the business to one of my friends and take my cut. I wasn't against bullying my way into the drug game either. I learned the ropes in my neighborhood where only the strong survive and hold their spot. The kids who sold drugs in that school did it to be cool. Looking back now, they were just young kids. They had no idea the evil that came with all that illegal money.

I only knew how to play the drug game one way, eliminate the competition and hit the streets running. Being able to see the potential in my new-found arena, I wanted it all. The school that I came from before, did not have kids with $50 and hundred dollar bills sitting in their pockets. I came from an environment where I spent my days chasing $5 and $10 drug sales.

I decided to bring my .380 handgun to school. I grabbed my football playing cousin Shane and Tom. They were just decoration and I didn't even tell them what I was about to do. I was on a hunt to find the hippie kids who sold drugs in my school. The hippie kids used to play hacky sack behind the handball wall and make their sales. This was the area the kids passed to reach the hangout in the woods where everyone would get high. I walked up to the two kids who were my competition and before they knew what was going on, I had pulled the small gun off my waist and used the weapon to pistol whip both peaceful kids. They had never encountered any assault of this magnitude. Other kids could see and this is what I wanted. I looked at them and said, "If I hear you are selling drugs in this school again, I am going to kill you." They said, "Chill out man, chill out."

When you let a wolf into the chicken coop there is only one outcome. This is how I approached the drug game in this school. If I did not believe that you were strong enough to withstand the pressures of operating in the underworld, then I'd be damned if you were going to take any money that I felt belonged to me. I wasn't a killer, but I wanted them to think I was. There were all sorts of rumors running around about me and I played them up. Shane was an athlete and good kid. I scared him more than the dudes' I was trying to intimidate. I had changed so much since we were little kids, and he did not expect the Jeff that arrived at his school.

Business was good for a fifteen-year-old. I was making more money than most of my friend's parents. The more money I made, the more I spent. I had all sorts of toys, dirt bikes, top of the line surfboards, jewelry and clothes. Grandma saw all my stuff but at this point it was easier for her to not know what I was involved in. I never asked her for money and she was fine with this. She was happy I was taking care of myself.

You couldn't tell me anything. I was going to school but never to class. I was enrolled but I just traveled around to study hall, the Commons and the hang out areas. I thought what could I learn in class? In my opinion, I had found my calling. The school would call my house but Grandma would always speak Dutch to the people she didn't know. Grandma spoke English just fine but she would play the "no speak English" card when she needed to. This kept the school and cops from telling her things and made it difficult for anyone who asked too many questions. If Grandma got caught speaking English before she knew who the people were, she just talked about my father as if he was who they were asking about. I loved my Grandmother for this. During World War II she had witnessed what people in power were capable of and she learned not to trust them. This allowed me to get away with a lot.

* * * * * *

Andy and I were making so much money for our connect that he finally wanted to meet me. Our connect was a guy from Brooklyn named Dennis the Menace. Dennis was one of the Godfathers of the New York Rave Scene and he had a LSD connect who was tied to the Grateful Dead Scene. Dennis was a pure genius. Dennis grew up with a DJ named Frankie Bones, a Guido who spun club music. Frankie hooked up with another DJ names Lenny Dee. Lenny Dee had come back from the UK with the Techno records that were introducing Electronica. Frankie and Lenny started playing with the sound and Dennis needed a place to push his LSD so he started throwing the first Raves. During this time, they were called "Stop Parties" The parties were underground and you really had to be in the loop to know where these parties would take place. By the time I was invited, Lenny and Frankie were throwing "Storm Raves" and it was the greatest thing I had ever seen.

Andy picked me up one night and told me we were going to one of the Storm Raves. On the way, Andy told me I was going to meet the guys behind the scene. I was told there would be rules about who could sell drugs while inside and he was telling me about Ecstasy. I had seen them in his dorm room, but I didn't know anyone who had even heard of this drug. I had drugs with me, and remember, I was fifteen and thought I was tough. I didn't take orders, I gave them. I was doing business with grownups and if this was our connects party, why should he care who was selling his work? Andy gave me a pink pill that looks like a "life saver middle" and I popped it and we were on our way.

We arrived at the warehouse where this party was being held and once we were inside, what I saw was incredible. The bass was pumping, the strobe lights were going off and there were girls and dudes who were fly as hell in styles like mine. I had heard Techno because Andy listened to it all the time but I was a rap dude. The Ecstasy was starting to hit me and I was catching a warm rush that made me feel so good, it was as if I was in heaven. Andy and I were walking around and he was introducing me to people who had these unique names and I told everyone my name was Jeff D, D for Delirious. Delirious was my first tag but I shortened it to Del because it was faster to get off when I was bombing. The drugs in my system and the lights were surreal and I felt like I was where I belonged.

Kids were doing drugs right out in the open and I saw sales going down. Andy and I were in this little area where they had couches called "the chill out room". Andy was talking to a woman named Joyce who was a promoter and worked in a trendy store in the mall. I knew her. I was looking around the room when I saw group of dudes with a Black book. A Black book is an art book and graf artists practice in them or collect the work of other artists they run into. I was watching dudes throw their tags in the book and I cracked a blunt, rolled up and took a couple of pulls. The weed began to kick the Ecstasy into full speed. I passed the blunt to the kid with the book and he passed me the marker and the book. I saw his tag "Sane". I looked at him hard and realized this was my old tag partner. I could tell he was fucked up and we hadn't seen each other in a while.

Sane was a New York legend. He was all over the place. He was a B-boy and graf was his life. When I lay my tag, I made sure I added Task Mob because this had been our crew. I placed the book back in his lap with my finger on my tag. Sane looked at my tag and looked up at me. We caught up and that's what these parties were about. They were networking for the elite and unique. While I was chilling with Sane a girl asked him if he knew who had tabs. Now I knew what Andy had said, but I didn't ever like to turn down money. I busted the sale and the girl must have told her friends because people started asking me for drugs so I served them. Sadly, Sane later died doing what he loved. He fell off a bridge while bombing and plunged to his death.

Back then the word traveled fast at these parties. The hits we had were called "Black Paradise". The books had pictures on the paper and this is how people knew what was good. All the Black Paradise books were coming through Dennis's connect, but I wasn't the guy who was supposed to have house rules. House rules back then, meant you had the ok to operate. I didn't have the OK to operate, after all, the boss had never met me yet, he had only heard about me.

Andy was walking towards me with a dude everyone wanted to shout out. Andy made it to me first because the guy he was walking with was talking to a group of chicks. I think Andy wanted to be pissed, but it was difficult due to the MDMA flowing through his blood stream. Andy was reminding me what he told me in the car as if I forgot. I didn't get a chance to explain how I didn't care or how I didn't feel the rules pertained to me because the man of the hour was upon me. "So, you're the wonder boy out in Long Island and the kid who is busting sales at my party." I had not made it this far in my short life by not being fast on my feet. I didn't care how fucked up I was, I knew I only had one chance to make my first impression. I was young and on the come-up. Without missing a beat, I looked at Dennis and said, "We are trying to buy you out Boss and I had to chase every dollar. How is this your party and everyone is looking for drugs? Someone isn't doing their job." Dennis looked at me and looked at Andy and laughed. I knew I had him, I was always good at reading people. I was patient, but I was going to get next to Dennis sooner or later. It ended up taking a little longer than I would've liked, but you'll see why. Life was going to throw some choices at me and as usual, I fucked it all up for a little bit.

For the next couple of months everything was good. I was making money, going to a Rave every weekend and I started dating Joyce the promoter. She wasn't as pretty as the other girls I was sleeping with, but she was 20 years old and someone who was in the Rave Scene. I was living a blessed life. Every once in a while, I would go to my old neighborhood, but my life was so much bigger than my old hood. I had a taste of the good life and I knew where I wanted to be.

I was busier than the average 15-year-old, but I always made time for Joy. One day we were hanging out at Grandma's and as I was making my gourmet meal of Chef Boyardee Raviolis, Joy was looking at the family photos on the dining room mantle above the fireplace. I walked over to Joy and said, "Would you like to have this picture of me?" Joy looked up at me with her cute little smile, and she simply said, "Yes." I took the picture out of the frame and gave it to her. I was certain Grandma would be upset later, but right now it was about making Joy happy. After Joy accepted her photo I gave her a light kiss on the cheek. I didn't make her my girlfriend because I didn't want to take her innocence. Grandma, my mom and Joy were pretty much the only good things in my life. Everything else was tainted in one way or another.

One of the kids Andy was dealing with from Kings Park got busted with a couple of sheets of acid. I knew the kid and I knew his Honda Accord because it was tight. The rumor mill said this guy had blown town after making bail. I had a friend named Joe I met at school and we would always go surfing. Joe's friend Brad had broken into the kid in Kings Park house and stole his car. They showed up at my house in the stolen car and Joe said, "Jeff, I have the alarm code to my ex-girlfriend's house and her parents keep $50,000 in the house and they have a bunch of guns too." The game plan was, we were going to rob the house, then take the stolen Honda that we believed wasn't reported stolen because the owner was on the run, and we were going to go to

Myrtle Beach. We wanted to go surfing but it was winter in New York. This all seemed like a great idea at the time. After all, what could go wrong?

Pauly D was a member of the team who dealt with the weed and coke. He would always drive me to school and drive me around. I trusted him more than I trusted Joe and I didn't even know Brad so I called Pauly and he was down with the burglary but he wasn't going to come to Myrtle Beach. Pauly came to my house and we all piled into his Dodge Shadow and headed to Joe's ex's house. We parked the car on the block behind the house and went in. Joe did know the security code, but the rest of his info was bullshit. There was only about five hundred bucks in cash and the guns we found were hunting rifles and a shotgun. We loaded up the car and took off. Little did we know, one of the neighbors saw the car and got the plate number. Pauly knew someone who would take the guns, but I wanted the shotgun.

The job was a bust but I wanted to go surf down south so I took five grand out of my stash to fund this adventure. Pauly dropped us off at Grandma's and said, "See you when you get back." Little did we know, it would be a year before I would make it back to New York.

FOUR

ENDLESS SUMMER

"Someday you'll realize the damage you've caused"
-Unknown

I loaded my two brand new surfboards, the wetsuits, skateboards, a bag full of clothes, a half-pound of weed, two sheets of acid, the shotgun and the Colt .45 I had along with a couple of boxes of bullets. Like I said, what could go wrong? This trip was "boys in the hood meets endless summer." For some reason, I felt the need to call Joy so I could tell her I was taking a trip. I didn't even call any of the girls I was sleeping with, but I made sure to call her. She made me promise to stop by her house on our way. I told her I would, but I never ended up making it to her house to say goodbye. I yelled up to my Grandmother and said, "We are going on a surfing trip!" She said, "Be safe and have fun." We got in the car and we were off. Years later, I would find out Joy waited in the living room by the bay window for me until she finally fell asleep.

We cranked up the Beastie Boys and we were on our way. I had Andy's driver's license and made sure I brought it with me. We didn't look alike, but I looked so strange most people didn't stare at me too long. Everyone in the car knew how to drive so we took turns and got high the entire way down. When we got to the "South of the Border", we pulled out our skateboards and a pilot marker. We all skated around and I was throwing up tags. We ate, played video games and bought fireworks. We got back into the car and we were on our way to the beach. Once we arrived, we found a hotel right on the beach. I used Andy's ID and paid for a week. The room only had two beds, but there was a couch. I was paying the bill so I would let those two figure the details out. We all fell asleep, it had been a long ride.

There was a nice break off the pier right next to our Hotel. Joe and I geared up because the water was still chilly, but the winter swells had brought in shoulder to head high sets and we were out there with a few dudes. I have always had an aggressive style of surfing. My style made me stand out in the water. Local surfers are usually possessive of their breaks, but I've never lived close enough to have a local break. Even New York surfers aren't friendly, but the Myrtle Beach kids were cool and laid back.

After we were done, we invited two of the kids back to the room to get high. We got to the room and Brad was awake watching TV. Anyone who has ever been around me for any period of time got used to the presence of drugs and guns. These things have always been around so I forgot that guns and large amounts of drugs make some people nervous. It was obvious our two new friends were nervous. When they walked into our hotel room there was a pistol, shotgun, cash and drugs sitting right on the coffee table as if all of this was legal. The good thing about weed is, after a couple of pulls off a blunt, everyone tends to relax. With everyone nice and high, it was time to find out what type of trouble we could get into. After all, we were on vacation.

We got directions to the mall and a few good places to eat. The boys also told us about this hot new club. They left the hotel room and it was time to get cleaned up and go exploring. When it was time to go, I threw the gun in my waistband, grabbed some cash and we were on our way. The mall had everything a young trio of teens would want. When we arrived, the mall was jumping and there were girls all over the place because there was a college nearby. We kept hearing about this club, it was called "Club Zero". We were told it was open on Friday and Saturday nights. Club Zero wasn't a Techno club, the club played Rap, techno and alternative music all on the same night. A little something for everyone.

Brad and Joe were both eighteen years old and had ID. I had Andy's ID and it said I was twenty-one because without ID, I wouldn't be getting in. In New York, I never needed ID because I would always be on the list, but I wasn't in New York. It probably would've been better if I had not gotten in. Friday was two days away and Joe and I surfed a couple of hours a day. The waves were good the entire time we were in Myrtle Beach. All three of us went skating and we met some kids at the mall who brought us to their halfpipe they had in the woods. We brought the guns and were blowing off rounds with the skaters. We were having fun and I sold acid to the kids we were meeting. We ended up bringing some girls back to the Hotel. A country accent to me sounds horrible on a dude, but sexy as hell on a girl. We partied with everyone we met.

Friday was upon us and it was time to see what this club was about. Club Zero was in a shopping center but by the time we arrived, the Quickie Mart and the club were the only spots open. The parking lot was loaded with cars and people. Guys were showing out and you could hear the systems bumping from freshly waxed rides. It was clear to us this was a hotspot just like everyone had told us. I had left the .45 under the passenger seat where I had been sitting but I brought some acid in with me because it was easy to hide. When the bouncer saw our Id's, he didn't pay mine any attention because he was from Brooklyn and was happy to see New York boys. We were in and he even gave us a wristband to buy drinks. The music was bumping and the club was really nice inside. We pulled up at the bar and started doing shots of Jägermeister. Anyone who has drank Jägermeister knows it doesn't take many shots to get hammered. With the weed we had smoked on the way there, and the four or five shots we hit back to back, all three of us were feeling good. It was time to hit the dance floor.

I made my way through the crowd and the DJ was playing his rap set. In the middle of the dance floor there was a battle circle and I made my way to the outer cusp, bouncing to the rhythm of the music. Due to the fact this club played a wide variety of music, the club was a melting pot. I had never been to a club that played three types of music all on the same night. In New York, clubs played one or two similar genres of music, but this club had to placate to everyone. I was making my way back towards the bar, still bouncing to the music when a cute cheerleader type girl came up to me and said, "I have never seen a white guy with dreads, can I touch them?" I said, "Sure." I was ready to spit my game when a steroid infused Guido grabbed the cheerleader. She was cute, but this was a club that was filled with all sorts of broads so I kept it moving. I could fight well but steroid boy was twice my size and I wasn't that drunk yet. I hit the bar, took two more shots and was going to see what I could get into. I ran into some of the people we had met the past few days and I made a couple of sales. I kept bumping into the cheerleader from time to time and would talk to her and her girlfriend.

I finally was back with my two travel partners and as the night progressed, I got drunker. I spotted the cheerleader and her friend who were both dancing with steroid boy. I made my way onto the dance floor and danced my way up to the cheerleader. She turned my way and started to dance with me. When steroid boy turned around and noticed it was me, he pushed me. I was drunk, but not fall down drunk. I bounced right back to the cheerleader and grinded up on her and she played along. This was heading in the wrong direction real fast. Steroid boy didn't feel that I was worth swinging on so he pushed me away a couple more times. The cheerleader girl was laughing and getting sluttier in her moves. Meathead pushed me real hard and I tripped over a person and went down. The cheerleader and Mr. Box of Rocks started beefing with each other. This guy had two chicks and I was just playing with the one that was coming at me. But it was obvious, playtime was now over.

As quickly as I had gotten up, I was putting together my plan. Brad and Joe had seen what transpired but neither one of them were tough guys, but they could follow directions. I got back to them and told Joe to stay in the club and watch steroid boy and when he came of out the club to let me know because Brad and I would be at the car. Brad and I left the club and went to the car and I told Brad to keep the car running and to make sure we had a clear line to get out of the parking lot. I pulled the .45 from under the front seat, cocked the gun and waited. Brad looked very nervous. I wasn't going to kill steroid boy but I sure as hell was going to shake him up.

Joe came out of the club and pointed out Mr. Box of Rocks as he was making his way with the two cheerleaders. I let them pass the car and I got out and started talking slick. When big boy realized I was talking to him, he pulled off his jacket. I guess he figured he was going to beat me up. The funny thing was, his stupid country ass couldn't see what was in my hand. When steroid boy started coming my way, I raised that hand cannon and when the parking lot lights hit the chrome, his eyes dilated like a crackhead when they take a blast. I had made enough noise that people were now watching. I double tapped the trigger, aiming way over his head, as all the steroids in his system gassed his legs into gear. I hit one more shot into a car window in Box of Rocks direction. The shattered window and the boom of three thunderclap shots, was enough to cause wild panic in the parking lot. It was time to roll and other cars were already getting out of there. I couldn't see Joe's face because he was in the backseat, but Brads eyes were wide and nervous. I had to tell him, "go, go" before he snapped back to reality.

We got out of there and I'm sure the cops showed up, but I had no plans of being anywhere around when they did. It was obvious Brad was freaked out by what happened. He managed to drive back to the hotel though. When we all got back to the room, Brad began to break down. I wasn't worried about much, I figured we were safe because we made it off the scene, but Brad was convinced we were all going to jail. Joe and I decided we would leave in the morning for Florida, but Brad wasn't going to be coming with us. It was time for Brad to go home.

In the morning, we dropped Brad off at the Greyhound Station and I gave him two hundred dollars. Brad caught the next bus to New York and Joe and I were back on the road. The game plan was to hit Daytona Beach and surf a little bit and then head to Ocala Florida to see my sister and father. I hadn't seen or spoke to my father in years and I missed my sister so I figured I would pop up and surprise them. Dad had fucked up with his rich wife and she was now his rich ex-wife. Dad's old farm was now his ex-wife's farm and it was located right off the highway. If I could follow the signs to Ocala, I could find my way to the old property and get directions from Dad's ex. I wouldn't need those directions though, because my arrival would make the news.

The ride from the Carolinas to Florida was smooth. Joe and I took turns driving and we smoked weed and drank beer the entire ride. We made it to Daytona Beach and it was night time so we wandered around the strip right off the beach. We didn't even get a hotel room, we just pulled up to the beach and fell asleep in the car for a few hours. When the sun began to rise, so did we. After grabbing a quick breakfast washed down with a little weed, we paddle out into the break. We surfed all morning and then wandered around some more. Daytona was cool but I wanted to see my sister so I told Joe we were going to Ocala. We should have left earlier but we were chasing girls around and didn't end up getting back on the road until sometime after 11 pm.

Ocala Florida is horse country and it is in the middle of nowhere. Joe and I were driving a tinted out silver Honda Accord with five star rims, two surfboards on the roof and New York tags. To get to Ocala off I-95 south, we had to take a stretch of highway they call Alligator Alley. Alligator Alley has patches of swamp on both sides of the Highway. I have always believed the only place a gator should be is either on my feet or around my waist. I am from New York and I am afraid of Alligators. The summer I was down in Florida, my father dragged me behind the boat water skiing and I was bent over with my chest on my knees because I saw Alligators sunbathing on the lake I was in. I couldn't hold on anymore and fell. I kicked the skies off and swam for the boat like I was Michael Phelps. Sharks I can stand, but Alligators are not for me.

I was driving while Joe caught some sleep in the passenger seat. I wasn't speeding, but a cop pulled out and got behind us. I woke Joe up and we both got nervous as the cop continued following us. I pulled the .45 out from under my seat and Joe looked at me frantically and said, "I think they have the death penalty in Florida." I said, "We aren't trying to kill anyone, we are just trying to buy some time so we can get away. This fucking cop has been behind us for a couple of miles. There is a bridge coming up and I am going to fire a few shots at the car." I had done this in the past in other stolen cars, and it had always worked in my favor. To verbalize these thoughts now sounds bat shit crazy. However, at the time, this seemed like a good plan. It was never a good plan, but it was the plan.

I engaged the cruise control, rolled the driver side window down and Joe grabbed the steering wheel to keep the car steady. I leaned out the window and aimed at the front grill of the police car and squeezed off 3 shots that lit up the night. I swung back into the driver's seat and hit the gas to disengage the cruise control. The entrance to the bridge was almost upon us, but we never made it onto the bridge because all I could see were flashing lights as four cop cars crossed from the other side and boxed us in. The officer had run the tags on the car and when they came up stolen, he was following us until his backup arrived. I would have run, but I was deathly afraid of alligators.

Joe just stood there in shock as the officer's bum rushed the car, smashing the windows out and yanked us out head first. When the officer looked at me, he must've thought I was an Alien or something because he said, "What the fuck are you?" He proceeded to throw me on the ground and let his dog bite my leg. I was face first on the ground just watching as they pulled out the shotgun, the handgun and all sorts of other illegal paraphernalia we had in the stolen car. God was once again on my side because they could have justified shooting us after I shot at them, but they didn't. We were in trouble for real. In 1991 in Florida, any person under the age of 18 was a minor. Joe was 18 years old so he was considered an adult. I was 15 years old so I was a minor. Minors who were arrested for serious crimes were not eligible for bail. Joe was granted bail and his family flew down and got him out. The last time I ever saw Joe was when I looked over at him in the other police car.

We had made the news, so I didn't have to find my father, my arrival was televised. Dad showed up and he was pissed off, but I believe he was more afraid of what was going to happen to me. I had a laundry list of serious charges, but I had never had to deal with the repercussions of my actions. The magnitude of what I did had not set in until I was sentenced to six years. Florida had good time laws and I would only end up doing nine months, but at the time of sentencing, I didn't know any of this. Six years to a fifteen-year-old, sounded like life.

After being sentenced I was sent to a juvenile penitentiary in Marion County located next to the adult's county jail. I was from New York and I didn't know anyone. Once I arrived, the officers shaved my dreads. I felt violated and was pissed off because I had always had my long hair. The other kids didn't know what to make of me. Some of these kids looked like grown men. The good thing for me was, I had been on the news and shooting at the police is like a badge of honor in any prison.

I made friends with a huge kid that came the same day as I did. He called himself KO. KO had been in a lower security prison farm in Jacksonville and had knocked out a guard, stolen a car and escaped. I have always known how to recruit muscle and in prison, you always need someone to watch your back. KO was a big dangerous kid and him and I would become best buds.

New arrivals were assigned a hall and each hall wore a different colored T-shirt or sweatshirt to signify your assigned housing unit. New recruits were not assigned cells right away. The first couple of nights you slept on a mattress in your cell blocks hallway. They called this "sleeping on the street." Juvenile prison is like camp, only this camp was for misfits. There were even girls in this prison. We used to get to hang out with the girls in the recreation yard and we saw them throughout the day in passing. Our days were structured with different activities, school, vocational classes and recreation. There were fewer female inmates and many fights over whose girlfriend each one would be. The girls were claimed as soon as they entered the facility. Don't get the wrong idea, we couldn't do much with them. You could steal a kiss occasionally, and maybe grab a quick feel, but some interaction was better than none for a bunch of horny teens.

The girl's hall had one boy who was assigned to their block because he was so small. The kid was twelve but looked like he was nine years old. The boy had shot his grandmother in the head because she told him he couldn't go out and play. The grandmother had lived, thank god, but the case was all over the news and the administration kept him with the girls for his protection. At the end of the day, you have different types of criminals. You have criminals who have no morals, principles or values, and then you have other men who live by a code of the underworld. The code of the underworld says, you do not commit crimes against people who are not criminals and you do not hurt women, children or people who are not involved in the game.

In the morning, every housing unit would empty into a Commons area and watch TV until their housing unit was called for breakfast and programs. I had only been in the prison a couple of days and the only friend I had so far was KO so I would play the wall and just watch TV. In prison, a man learns to feel the current of the population. When something is about to happen, a man or boy can sense the tension. This morning I could feel the tension. I was watching extra hard because I knew something was going to happen and I was right. A group of

Spanish kids from another housing unit got up and attacked a group of black kids from my housing unit and before I knew it, everyone was fighting. I watched the security guards hit the exits and lock the doors as they waited for backup from next door. My back was already to the wall when everything started, so all I did was swing on anyone who came within my arm range. The entire Commons room was in an uproar and chairs were flying along with fists and feet. This was the first prison riot I was in; however, it wouldn't be the last. Even with the alarms going off, I heard the doors click open. The officers rushed through the doors in full riot gear with their batons out and swinging. I caught a face full of pepper spray and a shot between the shoulder blades and my resistance was over.

Once the officers had each one of us subdued, they bounded our hands behind our backs with plastic zip ties. The officers were so good at this that we looked like the calves the cowboys rope at rodeos. They'd get us down, flip us face down, pull the zip ties tight and on to the next kid. Some of the kids were getting dragged out to get special beatings and they were placed in solitary confinement, also known as, "the hole". The thing with a situation this big is, everyone was involved and they couldn't put everyone in the hole. I didn't even have a cell yet that they could lock me in. They didn't feed us all day and we didn't go anywhere. I sat on my mattress with the rest of the guys who still slept in the hallway, and everyone with a cell stayed in for the day.

In the morning, everything went back to normal. When we came out to the Commons area, there were extra officers standing around in riot gear. This was the administrations way of letting us know if we acted up again, they would crack our heads open again. I was hungry and I didn't want any problems. I wasn't alone in my feelings and everything went back to normal.

After I had been there for a while, the counselors decided I wasn't a risk to killing myself and I was placed in a cell with another white kid. I called him Cowboy because he would tell me stories about his cowboy boots and sing country songs. We would wrestle most nights and I would always win, but he was ok. Our little wrestling fights were more like an older brother beating on his younger sibling. If anyone else had tried to put their hands on Cowboy I would have stepped up for him. Outside of the cell, Cowboy and I didn't hang out too much though because he was friends with the other country white boys and I didn't have anything in common with them. I hung out with KO and his black friends from Jacksonville. We would work out with the little bit of weights they had and listen to rap music. I would tell them about New York and they would tell me about their hood.

The prison had an art room and I would go in there and draw little graffiti pieces I would send to my sister or Joy. Joy was the only person from New York who wrote to me. I had not shown up at Joy's house like I told her I would, but I was able to call her. The first time I called Joy I was trying to explain why I never showed up, but she was talking so much, I couldn't get a word in. I think she was so worried about me by the time she heard my voice, she was just happy to hear I was ok. I felt it would be best to tell her the "PG version" of what I had went through. She had no idea I was ever involved with guns and she sure as hell wasn't going to know I was involved in a shootout with the police so I just told her the car I was driving in was stolen and I got in trouble. She was upset to hear all I had gone through, but she became really upset when I told her they had shaved off all my blonde hair. Honestly, she seemed more upset about the shaved head than anything else I had been through.

When I was on house arrest at my fathers, Joy baked me Christmas cookies and her mother sent them down to Florida. The cookies didn't taste very good, but they made me feel special. This would be the only Christmas gift I would receive. All my other girlfriends didn't write or do anything for me. Party girls don't stick around when there isn't a party. It would take me many years to realize the party girls were not what I needed or wanted in my life.

My father and sister would come and see me on the weekends when we had visits. The visits were held in the mess hall and we would eat and hang out for a little bit. It was cool to spend time with them and I was able to make sure my sister was ok. My father cared about me in the only way he could. The truth was, he was probably more damaged than me.

One day KO got into a fight with an elderly guard and KO knocked the old man out and the other guards jumped on him and put him in the hole. KO was in the cell punching the small thick glass window and flipping out. At night, the guards would pick a few guys and they would give us skittles or other types of snacks to do the cleanup. I was in my cell with Cowboy when one of the guards came to the cell and told me they wanted me to see if I could calm my friend down. I was given a broom and a bag of skittles. The guard let me into the block that held the hole cells. The cells in the hole didn't have anything in them but a cement shelf that was for laying down and a hole in the floor to piss and shit. The cells are hosed down and the light is left on twenty-four hours a day. Three days in one of these cells seems like weeks.

I could hear KO slugging the door the minute I entered the block. I pushed the broom to his cell and saw the small window covered in blood. I called to my friend, "KO calm down it's me." and the thud of his fists hitting the door stopped. The guys called me New York. He called out to me once he heard my voice, "New York?" as he started to wipe the blood off the window of the door so he could see me better. I said, "You need to keep calm, you're going to be out in two days." I took the skittles out of my pocket, poured half of the bag into my hand and slid the other half under his door.

Across from KO was this big white kid. The white kid was a bully who thought his job was to be an asshole to everyone. I didn't know of anyone who liked him. The white kid was in the hole because two nights before in the rec room he had cracked a kid who had one eye in the face with the pool cue while they were playing pool. The one-eyed kid never saw it coming because it wasn't called for and it was a one-way assault. The big kid saw me give KO the candy because he was watching us. We started yelling at each other. This is called gate banging because there is a gate between us and we could not fight. He said, "Give me some fucking skittles" I said, "Suck my dick, I am not giving you shit". He said, "I will see you when I get out tomorrow." I said, "I am from New York and I have never been scared of no pig farming hillbilly from Florida." Ko started screaming, "I'm going to fucking kill you" to the kid I was beefing with. The kid was trying to egg me on, but I went back to trying to make sure my friend was going to calm down. In the mist of them screaming back and forth, the cop came and pulled me out of the unit. The hole was a harsh punishment but the most I ever saw anyone stay in there was 72 hours. But those were 72 long hours. I went back to my cell with Cowboy and welcomed the escape that came through sleep.

In the morning when I entered the Commons room to watch TV before breakfast, I noticed they had let the big kid out of the hole. I didn't forget about our encounter the night before and my promise to see him. The big kid was standing with his back to the wall in the corner. I wasn't going to put off my confrontation with this kid. He was bigger than me, but I wasn't a punk and win or lose, sometimes a man just has to fight. I walked up to the big black guard who was sitting at his post and said, "I want 5 minutes with the big white kid." The guard must have thought I was just talking because he said, "Go ahead tough guy."

Before the big kid knew what was going on I was all over him. The kid was so big and I was scared but I used the fear to generate power. I wasn't going to give this kid a minute to build an offense. When I was boxing, my coach told me sometimes guys are going to be faster and stronger than you, but if you out work them they will be forced to be defensive. The advice worked in this situation. I was swinging as hard and as fast as I could until the guards broke us up. The fight was the talk of the prison because no one liked the big kid but no one had ever brought the fight to him. Everyone knew I was KO's little man but now they knew I could take care of my own business. Only the guys in the hole knew about the beef, but word spread how I had been disrespected and that's why I jumped on the guy.

In prison, a man's reputation is worth more than gold. I was loving the respect that came along with a victory against a kid who most guys feared. The big kid may have tried to get revenge, but KO was back in population and I may have been lucky the first time, but he knew he didn't stand a chance against KO and me together. I rode out the rest of my time and it was time to get out. I was to be released to live with my father and sister.

My father had split with his rich wife and was now living in a crappy town called Redick. Redick was the ghetto outside of Ocala. My father had rented a two-bedroom apartment in a small row house complex. The crack strip was on the next block. The town was really small and only had a few stores and a school. When I got out, my sister had a bunch of her friends over for a welcome home party for me. I didn't know any of the kids, but there were a few cute girls. My sister was a cheerleader and every straight man in prison would dream of a coming home party filled with cheerleaders.

Our neighbor had just come home from state prison and he was the local weed dealer and a friend of my fathers. Since my little run in with the cops made the news, my sister had told everyone I was a gangster from New York. I had turned sixteen while I was locked up and all the weightlifting had packed some muscle on my frame. I had the prison glow and the girls were interested in the new kid from New York who was a bad boy. I took to a girl named Trina.

Trina was from New Jersey and her family had just moved to Florida. Trina's house was the hangout house. Her parents were cool and if you had beer and weed for them, you could party at their house. I was on house arrest, but I didn't have an ankle bracelet or any other device to monitor my whereabouts. My parole officer was a black guy who would stop by the house once a week and he was nice enough. I was doing a little work with my father and the race horses and I had also been helping my neighbor sell a little weed to my sister's friends. The truth was, Florida was a much slower life than I wanted.

One week the parole officer showed up as he did every week prior. My father informed him that next week if he wanted to see me, he would have to come later because I would be working at the OBS racehorse sales, and we wouldn't be home until late all week. The parole officer told my father he didn't come to our neighborhood after dark. I heard every word the parole officer said and knew I could run around all night. Prior to this, I would come home at 9pm because I didn't want to go back to prison for breaking my curfew. My father was a heavy drinker and smoked a lot of pot and by 9pm he was usually passed out cold because he had to go to the barn to work at 5am. My sister could run around all night and Dad would never know.

I had met a kid named Jay who was from Chicago and he was a member of the "Gangster Disciples". Jay was more like me than the other kids in Florida. He sold drugs, wrote graffiti and missed the city life. We went out at night and threw up huge pieces on the few buildings in the small town. Jay was also selling weed for my neighbor but there wasn't really a lot of money in it for us. Weed is all over Florida. What we needed was some crack.

The block behind our apartment was the crack strip and Jay and I decided to go over there and explore. The crack strip consisted of small run-down houses and it was difficult to tell which homes were occupied and which ones were abandoned. The customers would pull up to the dead end of the street, click their lights and wait for the dealers to come from the woods. Once they saw the lights click, they walked to the cars and served the customers the drugs they requested. From what we could tell, all the guys selling crack on the block appeared to be crack users. Jay and I tried to find a cocaine supplier, but we didn't know anyone who could help us. We weren't going to let the fact we couldn't get drugs stop us from getting some of that money.

On that block, the dealers sold $50 slabs. We made up fake slabs with BR vitamins, baking soda, ammonia and food coloring. Everything we needed we got out of our local supermarket. The police had taken my guns but we got box cutters from the hardware store. We now had fake crack and weapons and we were off to get money.

The plan was simple enough. We would sit in the woods with the other dealers and when the cars would come we would back down the other dealers with the box cutters, come out of the woods and pass off the fake slabs. We wouldn't get greedy. We only needed to rip off a couple of people a night and we would be gone before anyone knew the stuff wasn't real. We pulled this scam off for a couple of nights. This plan was working out just fine. We weren't getting rich, but we were getting enough free money and that is the best kind.

Jay and I were up at the beverage/video rental spot drinking quarts of Blue Bull beer when a tricked-out Blazer pulled up. The tinted windows rolled down to reveal a huge black dude with a mouth full of gold teeth. The guy behind the wheel was called Heavy. He was the guy who moved all the crack in this part of town. Heavy said, "You Joe de Leyer's boy that shot at the police?" I said, "Yes" and approached the truck as Heavy said, "This is my block and I don't want to see you beating my customers." I said, "Just give the drugs to me and Jay and we will sell them for you." He wasn't trying to hear what I had to say. He simply told me, "Stay off my block." I guess that was a Florida threat. Jay and I both thought we were tough and in the Cities we were from, we would have gotten shot for what we were doing but this wasn't the city, this was a bum fuck town in Florida. We didn't pay Heavy any attention and we were back at it that very night.

The next night we were in the woods and it was my turn. We would jerk one or two cars each and then take off. The lights clicked and I came out of the woods and approached the Chevy Caprice. When I got to the driver side window I was looking at Heavy. I put my hand under my sweatshirt bluffing like I had a gun and walked backwards into the woods. I told Jay who it was and we cut through the woods back to the apartments. I thought Heavy was going to have someone shoot me, because this is what I would have done if I was Heavy, but that is not what he did.

The next day I came into the apartment and my father was drunker than usual. He was sitting in the chair when I walked in but once he saw me, he got up and starting ranting and raving and said, "I am not going to allow you to make the same fucking mistakes I did when I was young. The reason you are here is so you can get your fucking life together." I said, "How are you going to tell me what to do when you can't even get your own life together? You're a drug addict and a drunk." His fatherly advice to me was, "Do what I say, not as I do."

I was angry by this point because this man who had never been there for me my entire life, now felt as though he had a right to guide my life when his life was such a train wreck. Apparently Heavy had told my father on me and my drunk father was now flipping out due to what Jay and I were doing. Yeah, I was a fuck up but this was nothing new. By this point I was enraged and I walked up to him and said, "Maybe I wouldn't be such a fuck up if you weren't such a piece of shit father." My father took a swing at me and I hooked off on him. My father doesn't fight as well as I do and the fact that he was drunk didn't help him any.

We were both trying to get in position to fight and we were trying to get to an area where we could square up. Right before he came at me I pulled a box cutter out of my pocket. I was pissed and not thinking. My sister ran into the living room screaming, "Stop it, please stop." My father backed up the moment he saw the blade. I was moving into position to cut him when my crying sister got in-between us. The look on her face brought me out of my rage immediately and I stopped. My sister was only 14 years old and yet, she was expected to handle the chores of a grown woman. My father would get so drunk and high that he would pass out cold and my sister would sneak out of the house and go and do god only knows what with boys. I didn't want to leave my sister, but I had no choice. I grabbed my clothes and the box I kept my money in and I left.

I went over to Trina's house. Her parents liked me and they told me I could stay there. Not living with my father was a violation of my parole. The parole officer showed up for his weekly visit and my father didn't tell him what happened, but he did tell him I wasn't living there. My sister Heather told me that parole had come by the house. I knew they were going to pick me up but I didn't care. A few days later I came out of the supermarket and the cops and my parole officer cuffed me. I was going back to the Juvenile prison.

I got back to the prison and my friends who were still there greeted me. I was back to sleeping in the hallway again. I would only be there for a week though because I was going to a family court house to wait for my mother to come to Florida and take me back to New York. I had warrants in New York for the house we robbed that I would have to deal with, but I was never to return to Florida, which I would anyway.

I was taken to the family court house and the Sheriffs picked me up for transfer. When I was handcuffed and placed in the back of car, I started talking wild shit to the officers. The ride was a two-hour ride and these officers didn't want to hear my slick mouth about how lucky they were I was cuffed so they pulled the car over and hog tied my feet and hands together with the cuffs and placed me on the hump on the floor. I was really flipping out now as my face was all on the floor mat. The Sheriffs thought this was funny since I had told them what a gangster I was.

Once we arrived at the family court house instead of uncuffing me, they picked me up by my hands and feet that were cuffed together. I was trying to spit on them and promising to kill them. They opened the door with my head and dropped me on the carpet in front of the intake desk. All the kids in the house were watching this. One of the ladies who worked there saw this and went nuts about how they couldn't treat me like this and that she was going to report them. The officers explained I was an asshole and I deserved to be treated as I was. I was uncuffed and I talked a little more shit as they left. I had made quite the entrance.

The kids in this house were not criminals, they were kids who had family problems. I on the other hand was a criminal already. The kids that were there had clothes and stuff their parents brought them. I had lost all my clothes except for what I was wearing when they picked me up and my father wasn't about to come see me and bring me anything. There were about 10 kids in this place. The boys slept on one side two to each room and the girls the same on the other side. The kids were scared of me and I was shaking them down for stuff because I was on my own and their parents came and brought them stuff. I was acting like I was back at the prison until one night the black guard who I had asked if I could get 5 minutes alone with the big white kid showed up to work at the house. The guard pulled me aside and said, "If you keep acting up, I am going to beat your little ass." I chilled out.

There was a girl who was my age there. She kept running away from home and because she was not 18 yet, she had to be there. The house wasn't like prison. We could fool around and be together unsupervised. I had come up with an idea to sneak into her and her roommates room at night. The building was a flat ranch style house and in the bedrooms if you pushed the ceiling up there were I beams that ran the length of the building. The guard post separated the boys wing from the girl's wing. The plan was, once they did the lights out round, my roommate and I would crawl across the I beam into the girl's room and we would get some. This was a good plan until my roommate slipped off the I beam and fell through the ceiling right in front of the front desk. After that, they watched me extra hard because it was clear I was a troublemaker.

Mom finally made it down to Florida with my sister Charissa to get me. Charissa is four years younger than me and wanted to go to Disney World so mom rescued me and we all went to Disney. The plan was, when we got back to New York I would turn myself in for the stuff I was wanted for. Everything in New York happened before I had turned sixteen and in New York this meant I was a juvenile. Mom told me she would bail me out and I could get my life back together. Mom wanted me to go back to school. If I wasn't such a derelict, I would have listened to my mother and just tried to do the right thing, but this wasn't who I was. I was a young man who thought I had the world figured out so I told mom what she wanted to hear to get back to New York. I had my mind on getting back everything and more. I had been gone too long. The King was about to take back his throne.

FIVE

THE RETURN

"He's stuck between who he is, who he wants to be and who he should be" -Unknown

It had been over a year since I had been in New York and I had missed it. New York will always be my home and I might have fun being other places, but everything I have ever wanted is within reach in New York. The problem was I had warrants out for my arrest. Mom wanted me to turn myself in and I had agreed to do just that. In theory, turning myself in seemed easy enough, but actually walking into a precinct and voluntarily putting the cuffs on was a different story. All my life I did everything in my power to avoid getting locked up. I did it though. I got into the car with mom and we walked into the precinct. The lawyer had arranged for me to be processed and arraigned the same day. Mom posted bail and now I was warrant free. All I had to do was show up for my next court date and I would be ok.

The problem was, I was home and everyone I knew were running the streets. I missed my first court date and I knew the cops would be looking for me so I decided to go out to my Uncle's horse farm in the Hamptons. I knew no one would go looking for me there. Of course, this wasn't going to be a fun stay because my Uncle was going to force me to work. The work on the farm was hard, but I knew it so I did what I had to do to hide from the cops.

I wasn't in contact with many of my friends since I came back, but I was still speaking to Joy daily. Joy was one of the only people I spoke with from New York while I was in Florida. It had been a year since I saw her and I missed her, so I invited her to come out and spend the weekend with me. We never even kissed other than little pecks. She was such a good girl and I was a young criminal. I knew her mother wasn't exactly thrilled with the idea of sending her young daughter out to the Hamptons to spend the weekend with me, but Joy begged her mother for days. Her mother eventually called my Aunt and Uncle and they assured her she would be staying in the main house with them because I was staying elsewhere on the property. Eventually her mother gave in and Joy's aunt dropped her off in the Hamptons. Joy's mother liked me. Most mothers did. I was very polite and came from a very well-known family, but I was a wolf dressed in sheep's clothing.

Joy arrived on a Friday afternoon and she had a huge smile on her face the minute she saw me. Most girls loved horses, but she wasn't one of them but she pretended to like them because she liked me. We spent the day hanging out and talking while my Uncle worked me like a dog. I was staying in a little camper we had on the property and after I was done with everything I had to do for the day, we went back to the camper. I made us something to eat and we just hung out until we fell asleep together. I was a perfect gentleman on her first night.

The second night as we were laying in my bed, I leaned over and kissed her. Our kisses were different than I had experienced because they were soft and gentle. We explored each other's bodies with our hands as we kissed. I was experienced but I could tell she wasn't. I looked at her and said, "Are you a virgin?" and she said, "No." I knew she was a virgin even though she said she wasn't. She was so cute when she looked right into my eyes and lied. I cared about her. She wasn't like the other girls and although I wanted to have sex with her, I didn't want to take her virginity. This wasn't normal for me. At this point in my life I was trying to sleep with as many girls as I could, but Joy made me feel different. I didn't think I was the right person for her because she was a good girl, and I was nothing but trouble.

We did other things, but I made certain she would return the way her aunt had dropped her off. And she did. . .she left the next day. I had eventually left the Hampton's and was back in the streets shortly after our weekend together. We still talked on the phone, but our calls started to slow down because I was so involved in the streets and building a drug empire.

* * * * * *

In the time I was gone, the New York Rave scene had blown up. The parties were no longer small secret events but huge parties that attracted kids from all over. I still had money stashed at Grandma's so I retrieved the stash and I found out where the next rave was going to be. It was time to see what I had missed. Andy had retired from the drug game and he was finishing his degree, but he was still connected. I told him I wanted to go out and I needed to buy a couple of books so I could put everything back together. I was done selling weed. I had a taste of the hard narcotics money before I took my joy ride and I wanted back in.

Dennis and the Brooklyn crew were throwing a party on that Saturday and I wanted to be plugged in directly. If everyone was going to get on the rave scene bandwagon, I was going to move the drugs that went along with that lifestyle. When Andy and I got to the Brooklyn Armory where Dennis was throwing the party, I could see the change. The line was around the block. I had never seen so many kids in one place and they were all looking for drugs. I needed back into the game. Andy and I skipped the line because we were on the list.

Once we got inside the place was packed and the music was pumping. The Brooklyn hardcore techno sound was distinct. We were led up a set of stairs that put us where the lasers and DJ's were set up working the crowd. It was amazing to look down on the people and watch them react to the changes in the beats. I was dreaming of the possibilities when Dennis approached us and we embraced. Before I had left we were not close yet, but everyone in New York had heard about my little adventure and how I was back. I didn't waste time and I told Dennis, "I need to talk to you." He said, "Let's find a place with less distractions." With the loud music, this was difficult to accomplish, but we found an area behind the DJ station and sat down. I said, "Everyone looks like they're doing really well." He said, "I have no complaints" I said, "All I want, is what I feel I deserve." Dennis laughed until he looked in my eyes and saw I was dead serious. I told him, "I want my piece of the pie and I am going to take back what belongs to me. I want full control of the books that go to Long Island. I am going to put my crew back together and all I need is a supply line." Dennis said, "Let's meet up this week." We set a day for me to come into the neighborhood and now it was time to have fun.

The drugs were really kicking in now and I wanted to plot the setup, so I observed the party in action. As Andy and I started to wander through the crowd, we were running into all sorts of people we knew, and they were introducing us to all sorts of people we didn't know. Drugs were still being done right in the open and the days of assigned dealers was over because there were too many people. Andy and I enjoyed our night and I had done what I needed to do and saw what I needed to see.

Now that I secured my connect it was time to round up the troops. I started making calls and popping up on my old friends. Everyone was happy to see me and since I always had a plan to get a little money, the boys were ready to listen. The boys had some of their own things going on, but LSD and Ecstasy in bulk wasn't an easy thing to come by and I had the connect. I didn't miss a beat and it was time to connect the dots.

In Long Island a rave club opened called "Caffeine's" in Deer Park. I showed up with my crew and we locked the spot down. A friend of mines brother was one of the bouncers, and he told me all the bouncers liked to sniff coke, so we brought the drugs. I knew how to grease the wheels. I would pay the bouncers off with coke so me and my boys could sell our work. With the club scene taking off, there were all sorts of people showing up and I was going to make sure we would have what they wanted. In most bars and clubs, dealers usually sold $20 bags of coke. I took an ounce of coke and cut the shit out of it and made huge $10 bags. I would make sure my boys could sell their drugs for less than everyone else. I would make less but I would move more. I wanted the drug users to look for us and I was going to make my money regardless.

I had fallen right back into the flow. The problem was, I still had open cases pending. I wasn't putting all of this together to end up back in jail, even if it was only for a few months and probation wasn't an option with my lifestyle. I had to make a choice and I chose to say fuck the law so I didn't show up for court. Once again, I had another warrant out for my arrest. I already had a fake ID because I needed it to get into some of the clubs and I usually slept during the day. When I was in a car, I rarely drove because I was usually so fucked up on drugs, that someone else had to drive.

I had a BMW I bought but it was registered in one of my girlfriend's names. I went to clubs from Wednesday night straight thru Sunday. I was never in one place for long so the cops couldn't find me. I was now 17 years old, and I was living the vampire lifestyle. I was a creature of the night who lived in hotel rooms. I would buy my clothes daily and I lived off drugs and diner food.

* * * * * *

Dennis had eventually given up the drug game because he was the hottest promoter in New York, but as the scene grew, so did the tension. Michael Alig and Lord Michael had the Limelight and the tension started over who would control certain nights. (Michael Alig was later convicted of murdering his friend and dismembering his body. He spent 17 years in prison before he was granted parole. The movie "Party Monster" was a fictionalized movie about his life.) I was breaking my crew up and sending my guys to different venues so we could cover more ground. I had Matt and the guys I grew up with on my team so I knew I could trust them. The guys closest to me were guys I had spent most of my life with.

With Dennis out of the drug game, I was running into supply problems and I was buying up whatever I could to keep my guys in work. I was dealing with a guy named Jersey Jeff and he was dating a promoter named Liz. Jeff and Liz were part of the Limelight crew. Lord Michael and the Limelight crew had a good thing going and they were backed by big money. Everyone inside the Limelight was making a lot of money. The thing with the Limelight crew was, they were assholes who felt like their shit didn't stink.

One night in an apartment after a Disco 2000 party, we were all getting fucked up. Jersey Jeff knew I needed him to make my deals, so he got cocky and tried to talk dirty to me in front of his friends when he told me, "Go get me a fucking drink." I was the only one from my crew who was invited to come back to hang out so Jeff was feeling himself. I played it off and got on the phone. I called two of my friends who I grew up with and I gave them the address and told them to bring the guns.

Ivan and Richie showed up and were let in. Ivan handed me a gun and they followed my lead. Ivan was a stick-up kid and Richie was down for whatever. They came out to the club with me but they were hood boys and part of my goon squad. My boys followed me into Jeff and Liz's room where a small group of people were getting fucked up separate from everyone else in their apartment. Before they knew what was going on our guns were drawn and I said, "Let's see how tough you are now" as I cracked Jersey Jeff right in the mouth with my gun. He had used his mouth to disrespect me so I felt it was only right to smash him in the mouth with the gun. Liz tried to make a run for it but Richie grabbed her by her hair and said, "Where do you think you going bitch?" Jeff tried to get up from the bed to defend his girlfriend's honor, but one more crack in the head, gave him a better understanding how this was not a game. I told Jersey Jeff, "If you play games, your pussy ass will die tonight." The room was filled with people who did not try to rescue them. Little did they know, they would all be getting robbed. With everyone at gunpoint, we took what we wanted. This robbery was more about exerting a position of power than it had to do with the product and money we took.

As I exited the room, I told Jersey Jeff, "I wish you would try something because you and I both know, you're not like that. If I catch you and you look at me sideways, I will crack your head open again. Consider this the end of our arrangement, and the money and drugs will be my severance pay. Next time, go get your own fucking drink."

The best part of the situation was, no one in the other room knew what was going on so we took what we wanted and got out of there with the quickness. This wasn't one of my smarter moves because now I was blackballed. I couldn't get into any parties the Limelight crew threw and they cut off my line to Ecstasy and other club drugs they controlled. I was in trouble, but I wasn't going out without a fight and I wouldn't be locked out.

There was an unwritten rule that certain drugs (Crack Cocaine and Heroin) wouldn't be distributed within these parties because it would bring unwanted heat from the cops. The cops weren't concerned back then with Ecstasy, acid and special K. We sold coke and dust but the main drugs were Ecstasy and acid. Since I couldn't get the designer drugs due to being blackballed, I went uptown to Harlem to pick up dust, crack and dope. I showed up to the Rave on Saturday and started pushing the drugs that were a no no. The smell of crack and dust filled the air of the warehouse we were in. I did this two weekends in a row.

On that Monday Dr. Jay and Nicky Hollywood gave me a call and asked me to come into Manhattan and meet with them. Both guys were major dudes in the club drug scene. Dr. Jay would later get caught in Colorado and get a life sentence and Nicky would be killed in California by the Mexican drug Cartel. But all this would happen in years to come, during this time, they were both living the dream.

I told Matt and my top boys who I was going to meet. I would go alone, but if they tried any funny shit I needed someone to avenge my death, plus with a gun on my hip I figured I stood a good chance with anyone. I was still chasing a connect at this point and Jay and Nicky were dealing directly with real chemists. I was the man in my neighborhoods and the clubs, but these two guys were in the loop coast to coast. They were only a couple of years older than I was, but in my eyes, they were where I wanted to be.

I arrived at the Hotel, walked into the elevator and pressed 5 to get to the fifth floor. Because I was so cocky, I did a quick mental check and was ready once again to talk my way into the deal I was looking for. Ready to go, I knocked on the door and it was answered by a gorgeous girl who was so exotic looking, I couldn't even guess what her nationality was. I was lead into the living room and I was shocked by the setup of this hotel room. I had lived in hotels before, but they weren't like this. The nightly bill was probably the same as most people's monthly mortgage.

As I was led to the room where Nicky and Jay were, I watched with every step, the ass cheeks of the girl who was leading the way. When I got into the room, Nicky was on the phone looking like a fly Spanish rock star and Jay was sketching in his black book. Jay was a Filipino dude with long curly hair. He wasn't as flashy as Nicky, but he was still stylish. I walked over to see what Jay was drawing and I was very impressed when I saw his sketch of a warrior chick. When Nicky got off the phone, he came to me and we embraced. When he let go of me, he placed his hands on my shoulders, looked into my eyes, and said, "What are we going to do with you?" I laughed and he said, "Listen, we all have a good thing going but bringing in certain drugs can bring the whole entire scene to a crashing halt." I said, "I get it, crack and dope bring the cops but I am being blackballed."

I knew Nicky and Jay did business with the Limelight crew and I had been around both of them, but until this point, I had never done business with them directly. They chose who they dealt with and whoever it was had the power. Jay was just listening as Nicky continued speaking. I believe this is why they both worked so well together because they were different and it balanced out their business relationship. Jay would take everything in and process what a person was saying or not saying while Nicky did the talking.

Nicky was from the streets, so I put it all on the line for him. I said, "I think too many dudes are being put into positions they don't deserve, because if shit gets real, they're not going to be able to do what needs to be done. Even though we are selling designer drugs, we are still selling drugs and our business comes with dangers." During this time, there wasn't a lot of robbing and shooting in the designer drug trade. The clients were mostly kids with money and they were happy to find quality drugs. The rave scene was a gold mine and shooting brings the cops. All this would change in the next year or two, but at the time the parties were peaceful. Nicky said, "You don't have to worry about being blackballed because you are going to deal directly with us." Once again, I was back in the loop.

Nicky looked at me seriously and said, "You have to stay out of the Limelight. You can't send your workers there and we want you to leave Lord Michael, Jersey Jeff and anyone else associated with the Limelight alone. If you can do this, you will be one of the chosen when our shipments get into New York." I said, "Of course, I got you." I agreed for the sake of needing the connect.

We went out that night and it was really the rock star treatment. What people fail to understand about making money is, the more you make, the faster it seems to go. When you are trying to attract big clients, you have to flaunt your money so people are attracted to you and what you're trying to do. But just like any business, you must be smart because a couple of bad investments or unforeseen problems can cause you to lose it all. I was making a lot of money, but I was also a stupid kid. I took a lot of losses along the way. I would take off and go missing because I got on a plane and went somewhere. The only smart thing I did was show up at Grandma's house occasionally and put some money in my secret stash.

* * * * * *

At this point in my life, I was living in Brooklyn and traveling around Long Island every day. I had a good system because I had cells of ravers spread out all over. On the weekends, we would hit up all the different spots. I have always liked to travel and Philly is only 2 hours away from New York City. I had met a bunch of the Philly crew because I was doing business with a guy named Philly Dave. Dave was the Godfather of the Philly rave scene. He would later get killed by someone in his crew. He was a diabetic and someone close to him dosed his insulin.

The Raver lifestyle was spreading like wildfire and parties were popping up and down the entire east coast. The Summer of 1993 there was a three-day rave called Wild. The tickets were $50 a person and the party was held in Maryland on a campground. The party was promoted for months before it happened, and was talked about by everyone because it was the first of its kind. The lineup for the DJ's was power packed.

Pauly D and I were both dating girls from Jersey. The College FIT in Manhattan was a fashion school that had the largest population of raver girls I had ever seen and that's where we found the girls. My girlfriends name was Stacy and Pauly's girl was Jill and the girls were best friends. Pauly and I ended up on the Jersey shore the first night we met them. Because we had smoked so much dust, we couldn't remember how we got there or what their names were. But the girls were cool and in the loop so they lasted longer than most of the women in our lives at the time.

I was the type of guy who had 4 or 5 girlfriends at a time. During all my drama, I was still with Rachael when I went back to my old neighborhood. In my neighborhood, Rachel was my girlfriend and all the drugs were mine. At the end of the day, it was what it was. I felt like everything in that neighborhood belonged to me. It was a hands-off situation.

The whole Brooklyn crew would be there because Frankie and his brother Adam X were both on the line to spin. Pauly was going to the rave, but him and the boys were leaving from Long Island and even though I was living near them, I had decided to go with Stacy and her girlfriends from Jersey. I was bringing a lot of drugs and I felt better about my chances if the cops pulled us over in a car full of college girls, rather than a car full of dudes.

All the girls looked crazy. Stacy had dreads and a bunch of piercings, as did her girlfriends but they were still college girls in a car with Jersey tags instead of New York tags. I wasn't the smartest kid, but I knew how to transport drugs. The girls picked me up in Newark where I had taken the path train. I had a backpack filled with drugs, a handgun, one change of clothes and I was ready to go rave camping. Everyone was excited because the buildup for this party had been tremendous. The drive took about 4 hours and we didn't have any run in with the cops. So far so good.

We pulled up to the gate of the camping grounds and the cars waiting in line had license plates from a bunch of different states. At the gate, we handed over our tickets and were given a campsite number. We didn't have a tent, but a lot of people did. The sun was starting to set but it was still light enough to see the layout. There was a big field set up with a stage and a jumbotron that was flashing random images. A DJ was spinning and there was a pool with a bunch of people in it. On the far side of the field was a bunch of bathrooms and showers and behind that was the camping grounds where everyone was setting up tents. Along an inner road there were a bunch of pavilions set up that had clothes, food, drinks and other weird shit for sale and down the trail was an opening where another DJ station was set up.

The girls and I went looking for Pauly, Jill and the rest of the crew, but we couldn't find him. Later I learned Pauly had been arrested and he spent the weekend in jail. We found the rest of the crew and they had two big tents set up next to each other. We had converted the grounds into our own personal home base. We had a cooler filled with beer and the guys had a little barbeque going while I got the drugs ready for distribution. Dr. Jay and Nicky's LSD connect was dry at this moment, but Philly Dave had come through and all I had to do was find him.

I had enough old work to get started though so I broke everything down into assorted packages. All my runners had a little bit of everything and I tried not to give my guys too much at one time. If I wasn't at a spot, I would use a manager to hold the bulk of the drugs and money. Whoever played this position, was to find a corner and surround himself with people he knew. When the runners were finished, he would collect the money and give them more drugs.

The system worked well and I would use it my whole career. I had learned it from the boys back on the block when I was growing up. My strategies went so deep, I would even put all the runners in the same outfits so once kids did business with one of them, they could easily find my guys when they wanted more drugs. At Wild, we set up in different locations because the area was so big we needed to spread out and cover as much ground as possible. The tents had to be guarded because this is where we would stash the money until we decided to bring it to the cars.

The rave was off the hook. The music was good and they were shooting these really cool lasers in the sky. I had met up with Philly Dave and his crew so I had enough drugs, or so I thought. In the middle of the night, I was rolling hard on the Ecstasy and I ran off with two girls I had met on one of my trips to the main field. I slept with one of the girls and I never caught her name or remembered seeing her again. It was just that type of party. When the sun came out the party was still going strong. After a person ingests enough drugs, sleep is not an option and the drugs at this party were flowing. This party was our Woodstock.

During the day, they blew up one of the bouncy houses and brought this thing out called a gyrosphere. There were also chairs they called mind machines. In the gyrosphere, your arms and legs were locked in and you swung around in these crazy flips and spins. They had to keep hosing the things down because kids were throwing up. The mind machines were vibrating chairs. They had goggles that flashed colors and headphones that played trippy music and sounds. This party was a drug addict's paradise. I refused to go in the pool due to what I had witnessed and people were fucking everywhere.

At one point, I remember seeing the cops drive through the outskirts of the grounds. In plain sight are water bongs and tons of drugs. One kid even had a World War II gas mask hooked up with a weed bong, and when you hit the bong, the mask filled with smoke. The cops couldn't do anything because there were too many people so they left us alone. At a point during the day, I was back at the tent with my boys.

We were smoking dust and this hippy guy comes over to us and said, "These people were so nice to allow us to have this party on their property. Can you guys help us motivate everyone to pick up their garbage?" The guy even had a strange little dance all put together and he called it "the garbage pickup dance". Now everyone at this campsite was in the drug game and we were all New York kids who thought we were gangsters so we decided to fuck with the hippy. First, we passed him the sherm cigarette and got him good and fucked up. Once we knew he was flying high, my boys and I pulled out our guns and I said, "What would you do if we decided to hunt you like the movie with Ice-t." The hippy said, "Why would you want to do that to me dude?" He was acting scared but he didn't leave. The other guys jumped on the bandwagon and everyone was fucking with this poor guy, but he continued to hang out. He eventually left and playtime was over.

The party lasted three days and if I slept six hours in those three days, that was a lot. I had slept with three different girls, none of them the girl I came with. I pulled in a nice chunk of change while having the time of my life. I eventually headed back to New York with a girl I had been trying to sleep with. I didn't get her on this night either, but I did get to hug up with her for the whole ride home.

* * * * * *

Back in New York I rented a hotel room and slept for almost two days recovering. By the time I was back to what my normal was, it was back to the work week at the clubs. Jay and Nicky had pills for me and Nancy, Dennis the Menace's girlfriend, had Special K. I could always get coke and dust but I needed LSD. This was my number one thing and I couldn't get enough to keep up with my demand.

I needed to keep the sheets going to my guys so I needed books. I was calling around with no luck until I called a girl named Peanut. Peanut would end up hanging herself about a year after this and I never understood why. She was always so bubbly and happy but I guess we never know the demons people face when they're alone. Peanut wasn't a major player but she was getting some money and she had a good connect. When I called her, I didn't expect what was about to come. Peanut told me the connect had told her that he wanted to talk to me and we should meet at a club called "Bliss" in Manhattan. She told me the connect had known who I was and he felt it was time. I was excited as I always was when I was about to meet someone who could put me in position.

I went out shopping for myself and the two girls I was taking with me. The girls were new and their names were Heidi and Julie. They were two little raver chicks from Long Island who one of my boys put me on to. They were both cute girls and with a little bit of my help they would be superstars. Remember, part of my game was my appearance and arm candy is always a fashionable accessory. Peanut was a promoter for Bliss so the girls and I were on the list.

Heidi's parents were on vacation and she had their car. Like I said, two girls and a car made for safe travels. I had a backpack filled with drugs, money and a gun so I just took out a little work because I didn't have any of the boys coming. After all, I was out tonight to talk business. Before I left the car, I dosed the girls so they would have fun. We parked the car on the street and made our way into the club.

We got into the club and found a spot, this way I wouldn't lose them in the crowd. The drugs were kicking in and the girls started dancing. It was time for me to make my rounds and I was looking for Peanut when I see the "garbage pickup" dance guy from Maryland. I was shocked to see him so I went over and said hello. I even mimicked his little dance. I kept it moving though because I had important people to meet and I didn't have time to hang with the hippy.

A little while later, I finally found Peanut. Peanut told me that we needed to go upstairs to the VIP room and she would make the introduction. I went and checked on the girls and they were happy to see a familiar face. They were laughing and dancing and it was obvious the drugs had fully kicked in. I told them I'd be back and Peanut and I made our way through the crowd stopping to greet people along our route. The life of a club superstar is like the life of a presidential candidate. A lot of hand shaking with people who are just faces in a crowd.

It was show time once again to sell myself and show what I could do. We entered the VIP area and I was in game mode because I was about to meet the biggest LSD distributor of the entire East Coast of the 1990's. As I was escorted to the back booth my mouth dropped when I saw who was sitting there. I was speechless, and this was something that didn't happen often. The connect said, "Do you feel like doing garbage pickup now?" I was fucked up. I couldn't believe it was Hippy Joe from the Rave. I had clowned this guy and he was the one playing with me. I was the clown, and I felt like it at that moment.

Hippy Joe dismissed everyone at the table so we could speak. The time it took for everyone to vacate gave me a few seconds to refocus. Now that we were alone Joe said, "Not everything is always what it appears to be. Kid, you're getting a lot of money and you're moving up the chain, but all that rah, rah gun shit? You need to leave that alone. If you're going to get money with me, you're not going to bring the heat upon me because you want to run around like an idiot." I was stunned and said, "Ok." He said, "I knew who you were way before you knew who I was. I want to deal with you, but if you're going to be reckless, I can't fuck with you." Joe knew about me robbing the Limelight guys and he brought up the crack and dope stunt I pulled. He was telling me about myself. Joe said, "This isn't the time or place for us to discuss our business. I will contact you and we will meet up. Right now, let's enjoy the vibe of the party." Hippy Joe was a man who was in tune with what he believed to be the natural flow of the world. He believed what you put out was what came back to you. These were not concepts I was able to grasp during this time in my life, but I would listen and pretend I was interested as long as I could stay connected.

Joe was a chemist and a really smart guy. He was much smarter than I was. The way he had tricked me had me intrigued and I wanted to deal with him. This guy was a modern-day alchemist, but instead of turning led into gold, he was turning rye seeds into LSD that was worth all the gold. Joe and his partner Peter, a Greek professional snowboarder, were living with Donna who was Peter's daughters mother. Her family owned the biggest sod farm in Long Island. Joe told me he wanted me to come out to the farm tomorrow and we would talk more. He gave me a number to call and that was it.

I left the meeting shocked but ready to take over the world. I would now be at the big boys table and I could set the prices. I found my girls where I left them and although they didn't know what just happened, they could tell I was happy. We ended up dancing and partying until they closed the spot.

When we exited the club, we walked back to the car. The block we had parked on was the ho stroll of the West Side of Manhattan. Even though the sun was rising, the pimps and working girls were still out there. As we passed the pimp sitting in his Benz on the corner, we were just in time to watch Heidi's mother's car being towed away, with my drugs, money and gun by New York City's finest. As the car was being towed, the pimp got out of his Benz and delivered a pimp sermon straight out a Dolomite movie. Had this not been Manhattan in the 90's, I wouldn't believe that I was witnessing a true-life enactment of the pimp movies I had watched from the 70's.

Heidi broke into tears right away. She was on drugs and I'm sure her mother didn't know her car was being used as the rave taxi. I tried to calm Heidi down and she stopped crying, but as soon as Julie realized her best friend was crying, she began to cry and now Heidi was in tears again. On one of the best days of my life, I was stuck on a street hoping the police didn't roll by because here I was, with two crying white girls on the West side ho stroll of Manhattan. I looked at the girls and said, "I know where they are taking the car and I will pay to get it out." I needed to get them off the block so we walked to a diner that was a few blocks away.

I could eat because my life was about functioning under the influence of drugs. The girls however, weren't as seasoned. As I sat there and ate, they sat there and cried. When we left the diner, the sun was shining and we walked a couple of blocks to the impound yard. Now you must remember, I still had a warrant out for my arrest because I never went back to court.

When we got to the police impound, I tried to give the girls the money to go in and get the car. I didn't know if they searched the car and there were a few felonies in that backpack, not to mention the cops who were all around. The waterworks started again and they wouldn't go in without me because they were still tripping out. I knew the only way we were getting the car is if I went with them. After we paid and hopped in the car, I felt for the backpack and it was still behind the passenger seat. The three of us managed to get out of there safely.

I had to go to Long Island anyway because later that day I was set to go out east to the farm to meet up with my new best friends. One of them, I hadn't even met yet. On the ride home, Heidi explained how her parents were on vacation for a week and the only people at her house were her two sisters, one older and one younger. A house with no parents was better than a hotel. My car was at Grandma's house and Heidi's house was less than a half an hour away.

We dropped Julie off and went back to Heidi's. We fooled around and fell asleep in her waterbed. Heidi's bedroom was in the basement so it was perfect for a guy who slept during the day because it was nice and dark. Suddenly, Heidi's bedroom door opened and the light flooded the room and woke me up. I saw a dude's face and before I knew what was going on, Heidi's little ass was out of the bed chasing whoever the guy was. I threw on my sneakers, took my gun out of my bag, tucked the gun in my waistband and threw my shirt on. I made my way up the stairs and I could see Heidi and the kid arguing on the front porch. No parents were at the house, so I helped myself to the fridge.

Heidi's younger sister was in the kitchen and she wasn't paying me much attention. I looked at her and said, "Who is the guy your sister is beefing with?" She said, "That's Heidi's boyfriend and he just came home from the County jail." Now my childhood boy Chris had passed the girl off to me and I didn't know this girl had a man, not that this ever stopped me. I thought it was funny and so did the sister. I was about to make it even funnier. I stepped out the front door and said, "What the fuck is your problem?" He said, "The problem is between me and my girl!" I said, "She wasn't your girlfriend last night. How about you get the fuck out of here!" Just to drive my point home, I lifted my shirt and let him get a look at the reason he should do as I said. He did the smart thing and took off.

Heidi and I went back into the house and I made breakfast for us, even thought it was mid-afternoon. I didn't press her about her boyfriend because I didn't care and I think this turned her on. When she climbed into the shower I stripped and got in with her. This was the beginning of an on again off again lust affair.

I made the call to Joe and I put Heidi on the phone and she took the directions down. After all, she was the one driving me to the meeting. Heidi was a relatively normal girl and when I met her, she did a little partying, but being with me would change her life. Looking back on my life now, I am sorry for the life I introduced some of these girls to, but back then, I didn't care about anyone but myself.

The sod farm that Joe, Pete and Donna lived on was way out on Long Island right before the Hamptons and located in the middle of nowhere. The farm was huge and they had a beautiful little house that was behind the barn. They had turned this into their personal play house. When we arrived, Heidi went with Donna so I could talk to the guys. When I was introduced to Pete, I realized I had seen him around but I hadn't a clue who he was. We bullshitted for a little while and then they said we should go surfing before we talked business. I was confused, but they knew I surfed so I agreed to go.

We loaded up the car with Pete's surfboards and he lent me a pair of board shorts. I left Heidi with Donna and we headed out on our 30-minute drive to Road K on Dunne Road. Joe stayed on the beach while Pete and I paddled into the surf. Looking back, I think they wanted to put me in the water to make sure I wasn't tapped. I also now believe this is the same reason he didn't want to speak with me at the club. We surfed for a few hours and headed back to the house to talk business.

When we arrived back at the house, the guys showed me the lab they had set up in a greenhouse where they also grew exotic weed. Joe lit up a joint and it tasted like coffee. I knew it was serious when it expanded the minute it hit my lungs. As we were smoking the joint Pete said, "We only spend four months a year in NY because I am on the snowboarding circuit. Your books will come through the mail and all money will go through Donna. You are the only person who we will be dealing with in bulk, and the print on your books will be yours alone."

All of this wasn't just talk because they were ready for me right then and there. They believed it was important not to oversaturate the market. From time to time, they let things go dry and this caused customers to miss the drugs. If what they wanted was always available, it wouldn't be special. Pete said, "If you fuck this up you will be cut off and replaced, but if you hold up your end, we will treat you like family." I said, "I'm not going to fuck up."

These guys didn't need to sell drugs, but they felt like it was their obligation to produce good LSD so the club kids could expand their minds through the journey of a good LSD trip. In the time I dealt with these guys, I had never saw them with a gun. If someone was to burn them on a deal, they would just write them off. I was given a couple of names of people who no matter how much money they came with, were not to get anything and if they were to end up with my drugs, I would be cut off. Later in my career I should have used more of their strategies than my gangster ideologies, but I also wasn't able to manufacture drugs from nothing.

* * * * * *

The 90's were a violent era in New York. The rap music I listened to glorified violence and as young men, a lot of us were trying to live out these rap artist's words. The movies produced romanticized the villain and drug lords. Americans have always loved the bad guys and these factors had negative effects on my life. I was guiding my life choices by my culture and the fantasies of music and movies. Simone Signoret stated, "I must be careful and not do too much acting, because there is always the danger that I may forget my own life". This was the case with me. I played the role of what movies projected a gangster to be and this is what my life became.

The positive guys in my life like Joe and Pete weren't around long enough to rub off on me. When I was doing business with Joe and Pete, I was living life for the love of good experiences because these guys didn't glorify or approve of violence. Joe, Pete and Donna were about having fun, and selling drugs gave them the freedom to do whatever they wanted. They also believed it wasn't a party if they couldn't include their friends. Pete and Donna had a daughter and the baby would always be with them, even at the Raves. This wasn't good parenting, but the Rave scene was like the "Grateful Dead Scene" and their daughter was born of it. Donna was a strong believer in free love and Ecstasy.

One time the trio threw a private invite only party for the A list of the club scene. I had decided to bring a Spanish girl from the hood with me. This girl had never done more than smoke weed and do a little drinking, but she was cute and I made her up in the little raver chick style. We drove out to the farm and Donna was in the driveway with glow sticks and a big bag of Ecstasy. Every person who arrived at the party had to take a hit of Ecstasy. The girl with me looked scared and Donna looked at me and said, "She can't come in unless she pops the hit." The farm was too far to leave and I wasn't about to miss this epic party. The girl was nervous about how she would feel and what she had gotten herself into coming out with me, but I eventually got her to pop the hit.

The first thing she saw when we entered the Playhouse barn was a corner filled with mattresses, porn playing and people fucking. She was squeezing my hand so tight she almost broke my fingers. There was a huge trampoline in the middle of the barn and the techno was blasting as different top DJ's were taking turns showing off. Hippy Joe had on a top hat, and was rolling joints that were a foot long each. All the drugs and food were compliments of our hosts. We barbequed during the day, sleeping if we could, swam in the pool and hung out in the hot tub. The girl who had come with me, who was so nervous, was now skinny dipping in the pool, eating more Ecstasy and fully in love with the vibe of a scene she once thought was full of weirdos. We were all weirdos, but there was a freedom in being weird. The party lasted two days.

The rave scene was about embracing your strange. When the scene started the collection of us were skateboarders, BMXers, surfers, graf artists and other outsiders from the jocks and cheerleaders. However, as the scene grew we welcomed the supreme outcasts because the world's freaks needed a place where they could feel at home. In the Limelight, Michael Alig had a friend they called Jonathan the Junky. Jonathan dressed up like a baby and was in a huge playpen and he begged for drugs. It was not unusual to see people dressed up in the most elaborate costumes or to see six foot drag queens in full drag with platform shoes.

The scene was blowing up and guys I came up with were throwing parties and getting paid. Graff artists were designing flyers and finding work in other commercial art fields while other kids were booking DJ jobs. I was making good money selling drugs even though with more people came more competition. But the sun doesn't shine forever, and with the popularity of our scene came the FBI, DEA and local cops. Joe and Pete got hot or believed they were and disappeared. Donna and the baby were still around, but she said she didn't know where they went and I didn't believe her.

When it rains, it pours and I found myself having to make my way once again. I had lost the best connection I had and my lifestyle was eating up my money. I needed to figure something out fast or my time at the top would be short lived. The boys and I would go out and move whatever I could get my hands on, but the luxury of being the connect was over for the time being. Around this time, Nicky was killed in LA, Jay was in Colorado where he would eventually get caught, Pete and Joe were on the run and Dennis had retired from the drug game. Things were bad and they only got worse.

SIX

BACK IN THE HOOD

"The more things change, the more they are the same" -
Alphonse Karr

I was in the old neighborhood where I had gotten back into selling coke and weed to keep money coming in. But due to my warrants, I had to move from house to house and stay out of sight because Timmy the Terminator was now in charge of narcotics and he wanted me bad. The BMW was gone and I now had a Cadillac. Andy and I were standing outside of my car across from the local VFW in front of an abandoned house and Andy had a gun on him. I was clean because if I got picked up, I wasn't trying to add to my felony count. I saw the undercover car before it was on us. I alerted Andy and he threw the gun into the overgrown yard of the abandoned house. I should have run, but I wasn't sure if they were going to stop. But they did and Timmy was in the car.

The cops ran us through the regular pat and frisk and questions. It was always the regular routine. I start yelling, "This is some bullshit! I don't know shit and no, you can't search the car." I was starting to think that maybe they didn't know about my warrant so I was getting lippy about them always fucking with us. Timmy hadn't retrieved the gun, so he must not have seen it because the gun would give them probable cause to search the car. I was feeling pretty good like I might not be going to jail today, but this wasn't the case. Timmy was playing one of his little games and as soon as I started feeling like I had some hope, Timmy walked into the yard and picked the gun up and said, "Whose gun is this?" Andy and I both played stupid and Timmy said, "de Leyer, this is going to be your gun today since I am already taking you in for your warrant." Knowing you're about to go to jail has a way of dampening your good spirits.

I was taken to the precinct and because of my bench warrant, I would have to be arraigned before I could post bail. My lawyer was there right away. After all, my crew and I were very good clients. My lawyer did his job. He got me bail and I was out. When I got out, the lawyer called me and said, "Do you plan on showing up to court?" I told him the truth and said, "Paying bail as far as I am concerned is paying to get out of jail." They could keep the bail money because I wasn't coming back until they caught me again. This ideology is why later in my life, I was never granted bail again.

I was out and with this new change, I was charged as an adult. I was back where I started. I was back with the guys I grew up with, I was back with Rachael, even though I was still sleeping with Heidi and I eventually started sleeping with another girl named Karla. Karla was another neighborhood girl. She was a pretty blonde haired blue-eyed girl who resembled the actress Jenny McCarthy in her youth. Karla had problems at home and those problems caused her to run away. She often found herself in the streets, the streets that belonged to me once the lights went off. As a man of the night, the pretty girls knew if they ended up with me, I would make sure they were alright.

Karla became one of these girls. At night, she would be with me and when I was around during the day, she would boost clothes and god knows what else. Even when I wasn't around, Karla was good because she was looked at as one of my girls. I used to hear rumors how she had another dude she was messing with, but I didn't care because I had other chicks. Karla would bring me clothes and little gifts that I thought were cute.

I was in the cut behind a building with the boys one night because the block was hot, and Karla showed up with her friends. She said, "Do you want to get pizza?" I said, "Sure." When I went to give her money she said, "I got this." And they left. About a half an hour later, Karla's friend came running back to where we were posted up and told me quite a tale. The young girl explained how they went to the pizza place and how Karla bit the electric cord and got knocked out. I didn't mean to laugh, but really? Come on. The girl explained how she waited with Karla until the ambulance arrived and she told me what hospital they took her to.

I ended up getting a ride to the hospital and when me and my boys walked into the emergency room, we saw Karla's parents. Karla's father and I already had an issue when he once tried to force her in his car. As soon as her father saw me, he started to make a scene telling the officers all sorts of nonsense. If he had told them the truth, I may have gone to jail. Eventually, I was able to pass off my contraband, and made it inside the hospital room to see Karla.

Karla was awake and her teeth were black. I said, "What the fuck were you thinking?" She said, "I was trying to scam for free pizza." I guess she didn't realize how serious those volts were, until they dropped her. Karla told me they decided to keep her for a few nights for a mental observation. I looked at her and said, "Do you want to stay?" And she said, "No." I said, "I will come back tomorrow and get you when they have visits." The next day armed with some of her clothes, I came and got her before her parents could snatch her up. Karla was free and we went back to our normal routine. Lucky for her, the black shit came off her teeth.

* * * * * *

Back in the hood, guns and violence were now the way of life for me once again. One night the boys and I went to a hip-hop club and we were in the club deep because it was in our neighborhood. My childhood friend Chris got into a fight over a girl so we jumped the guy and the fight turned into a big brawl. This resulted in all of us getting kicked out of the club. We were all drunk and high and someone knew where the guys lived, so we piled into two cars and went to the house. We shot the front of the house up and smashed the motorcycle that was in the driveway. We all took off and went back to the apartment that a few of the guys were living in together.

A group of us were standing in front of the building hanging out drinking and smoking when we saw a car kill their lights and speed up. I pulled the gun out of my waistband and as soon as I saw the muzzle flashes light up the night, I started to fire. Mind you, I hadn't even been out of jail long enough to have a new warrant for missing court yet. I got a couple of shots off before I felt a donkey kick to my arm followed by a severe burning pain. I was shot. I had been stabbed in a fight as a kid and didn't know it until after the fight, but when I got shot, I knew it right away and it hurt. The bullet went into my right inner bicep and stopped when it hit the bone. Today, I can grab the bullet because years later it would push to the surface surrounded by scar tissue. I keep it in as a reminder.

I went to Marry Magdalene Hospital and was told removing the bullet would do more damage. I was stitched up and questioned by the cops. I told them I was walking past the building and caught a stray bullet and I didn't see who did it. The cops didn't believe me, but they knew how this went. Plus, it was less paperwork. I was having a rough time. Like I said, when it rains it pours.

Karla was still in the streets and the more she ran, the more she got involved in the streets. The oldest Dowling brother Nick was pulling safes around this time. Nick only hit commercial spots. During a PC Richards heist, Nick used Karla as a lookout and she didn't do a very good job because they all got caught. During this time, I was running so hard in Manhattan, it was months before I knew what happened. Karla had made a deal with her parents, if they bailed her out, she had to go to Texas. The law didn't really have her and Nick and his partner took the rap. They were the ones the DA wanted anyway. Once she was bailed out, Karla left New York.

I had eventually gotten into more trouble in the neighborhood and the authorities were onto my whereabouts. I continued to disappear into the club scene, but I would still come into the neighborhood and stay hidden in different houses. Most of the time, I would see who I had to and be gone before anyone could tell.

One day I was at one of the boy's houses hanging out, and Randy who was Karla's sister was in the house. We were all hanging out, smoking and drinking. After we were all high and drunk, Randy showed me a picture of a baby. I asked her, "Whose baby is that?" Randy said, "This is Karla's baby girl." I was taken back. I said, "How old is the baby?" Randy said, "A few months old." As I sat there doing the math, Randy said, "That baby looks a lot like you!" I was shocked, and my natural instinct was to deny so I said, "Babies look like everybody."

My mind was racing and I was wrestling with the thought of being a father. I could barely take care of myself. I thought I was grown, but I wasn't. I asked questions and learned she had married a dude in the military and they were down in Texas. I asked Randy, "Does he think the kid is his?" Randy said, "He knows the kid isn't his." This should have been the day that changed my life, but I was very young and dumb. I thought about the baby every single day, but I just couldn't change. I wasn't sure if I was the father, but there was a piece of me who wanted to be the father because I needed someone to love, and I wanted someone to love me.

SEVEN

ON THE ROAD AGAIN

"When one lives attached to money, pride or power, it is impossible to be truly happy" -Pope Francis

I had been traveling up and down the East Coast to visit different City's and their clubs. In a club in Manhattan, I met a gypsy kid named Eric from Cherry Hill New Jersey right outside of Philly. Eric was a really good artist, he was a DJ and one of the strangest kids I've ever met. If you have been reading, you know this isn't a small fete. Eric kept telling me how I needed to bring some drugs down around his way and we could hit the clubs. He said Philly was an open market. With Philly Dave now dead, I didn't have any connections in the city of brotherly love.

At this point, I was working with a team of girls. I still had my crew of guys, the ones I grew up with, but with my major connects gone, I was back to a bunch of runners and hand to hand handling my work. My girl crew was all of Heidi's friends and they got the job done. Eddy was a guy who lived around the corner from Heidi. Eddy had a tricked-out Jeep Wagoneer that was the rave mobile. Eddy would later

OD and die, but he was alive and well for this mission. Eddy picked everyone up and we trooped to Jersey, picked up Eric and hit the first club. I had drugs and as usual, I brought a gun. Eric didn't really have juice with the doorman, so I had to leave the gun in the Jeep, but if anything went down, I could get to the gun as soon as I got out of the club. I wasn't known in Philly and we were selling drugs and someone might try to rob us.

In the club, Eric and I made the sales and I would give the money to Heidi to hold. I didn't want the drugs and the money on me in case I got caught or something happened. We hit two different clubs and we did alright. The clubs were small but the customers were happy to find LSD and Ecstasy. We also had dust, but Eric and I were smoking that. In Philly, they had dust and the bags were only $5. In New York, they were $10 but the dust was not good so we just moved the other drugs. Eddy was on a hit of acid and was smoking dust with Eric and me. This combination of LSD and PCP was enough to melt the brains of even the most seasoned drug addict.

Eric was going to move to New York so he could live with me. I was going to find work for Eric as a DJ and promoting party's. We needed to get Eric's bed, records, clothes and turntables from his house. The case that a DJ's turntables and mixer are encased in is called a coffin. Eddy and the girls were in the Jeep that was parked in front of Eric's apartment complex. Eric and I came downstairs and told Eddy, "We are going to put the mattress and coffin on the Jeep's roof rack." The drugs that Eddy was tripping on had him in another world. Eddy said, "You are the devil and you are not putting a coffin anywhere near my jeep." I knew Eddy was flying high but I was tired and trying to get back to New York. I didn't have time for his nonsense. I punched Eddy in the face and Eric and I dragged him out of the driver's seat. We roughed Eddy up until he said, "Ok fine, you can load the jeep."

Eric and I ran upstairs to start bringing his stuff downstairs. Eric's bedroom faced the front of the building where the Jeep was parked. I looked out the window just in time to see the Jeep speeding out of the parking lot. Eric thought this was the funniest thing ever. I was convinced Eddy wasn't stupid enough to leave us, but I was wrong. When we left the club, I had grabbed the gun and put it into my waistband, but Heidi still had all the money.

So now I was stranded in New Jersey with a couple hits of Ecstasy that we hadn't sold the night before, a couple of bags of dust and no money. I asked Eric, "can we borrow some money from your mother or sister?" He laughed and pointed to the padlock on his mother and sister's door and said, "Welfare checks aren't due for at least another week. No one in this apartment ever has money." I told Eric, "Why don't you make some calls and see if we can sell the Ecstasy to someone." Eric said, "If you don't have crack or dope, we aren't going to get any money in this neighborhood. We have to wait until night time and then we can go back to Philly and sell the pills." We had two choices, we could pull an armed robbery or we could try Eric's plan. We caught a couple of hours of sleep, took showers and even managed to find something to eat. I was plotting the things I would do to Eddy once I got my hands on him.

Eric had a collection of rave flyers on his wall from parties he had been to. Eric had an idea of how to get us into the club for free. You must remember, I had a firearm on me I wasn't about to leave in Eric's apartment. It was rumored that Eric had made it to California and lived there a couple of months and made it back with no money. Eric was a gypsy and a con artist so he always managed somehow.

We jumped the turn style and got on the train that went into Philly. Eric took me to an Asian club that played Techno music. The club wasn't opened yet, but the crew was in there setting up. Once we got someone to open the door, Eric started fast talking and we were led to the owner's office. Eric showed the Flyers for different raves and claimed to be the promoter. The sales pitch was, we were interested in using the club to host big raves but we were interested in how the club ran. I would later do this and be serious when I started throwing my own parties, but on this occasion, we needed to get in the club without money and with my gun. We pulled off the first part of the plan. We were inside and my gun was on me. The owner was interested in what he heard so far and he said for us to hang out for the night. We received a tour of the whole place and Eric even went into the DJ booth and played around. Eric was a good DJ, but he was the best bullshit artist.

Not only were we in a spot where I was going to be able to sell my pills so we had money to get home, we also had free run of the spot and free drink cards. Eric came in handy every once in a while. However, he would fuck up the night. The door was open and there was a nice crowd who were mostly Asian, but there were all sorts of other people. The DJ's weren't that good and Eric even got in the booth and hyped the crowd up. I had gotten rid of all the pills so we now had money.

With business done, Eric and I smoked one of the bags of dust and started drinking. Eric could be a bit of an asshole and he couldn't fight his way out of a wet paper bag. Now I don't know exactly what happened, but I came out of the bathroom and a rough group of young Asian men had Eric surrounded and it looked like they were about to use Eric as a punching bag. There were too many of them for us to fight so I pulled the gun out. All of this took place at the main bar and the sight of the gun brought panic to the crowd. I managed to get Eric and we made our way to the door. The crowd of guys who wanted to kill us seemed to be growing, but no one was getting close enough. The bouncers at the door got out of our way and we made it outside.

Once we got outside we both knew we needed to get missing, so we ran all out until we made the corner. When we made the turn, I let off two shots in the air with hope this would prevent anyone from chasing after us. We ran for a few more blocks and I had to keep the gun in my hand because we were running, plus it was now hot from the shots. With some distance between us and the club, we pulled up in an alley and caught our breaths. I started pressing Eric about chicks. This was home turf so he needed to find some place for us to go. I had money to get us home, but we couldn't catch a bus until the morning and I wasn't really trying to go back to Eric's apartment.

Eric was not a lady's man and that may have had something to do with the fact that he was subject to rob your house if you brought him home or if you left your pocketbook where he could get to it. Eric tried a few numbers and it wasn't looking good until he called a girl named Crystal and she said we could come by. All of Eric's girls looked like dogs, so I knew not to expect anything special.

Eric and I took a taxi to a brownstone on the south side of Philly. We walked up the three stairs and rang the doorbell. The door was answered by a girl and she looked like a video vixen. Crystal let us into her house and the inside was really nice. We started to small talk and Crystal explained how she had three roommates, but none of them were home right now. I was on this girl. I was bragging about who I was in an attempt to impress her and even though I was still in my clothes for two days, I was still fresh.

We started smoking dust because Crystal had told me she fucked around. We were getting fucked up and I noticed she saw my gun. She didn't say anything about it, but she did see it. I brought up Philly Dave and she explained they had been good friends and she even told me information I wasn't aware of. I wanted to fuck this girl, and I was laying down my best game and it seemed like she was receptive, that is until she got off her phone.

Crystal had been on the phone with a low-level dealer that was part of the Limelight crew. Crystal was the Crystal meth connection, her father was a biker and they were cooking up meth, and her crew of guys who worked for her moved the meth. The guy on the phone was one of her New York connections. The guy didn't want me to know, so he used what he knew about me. 'He's probably got a gun on him' of course I did, I always did. 'He's probably smoking dust' I was always smoking dust. The kid convinced her I was planning on robbing her so when Crystal got off the phone with son from New York, she called her black boyfriend Damion who lived only a couple blocks away. Crystal told Damion that Eric had brought a kid from New York who was dangerous and they might be there to rob her. The fact that she had seen the gun meant the kid on the phone may have been right. Damion said he'd be right there. I didn't know this girl was anything other than a cool girl who happened to be hot and I wanted to fuck. But when she got off the phone in the kitchen and came back into the living room, I knew something was up. We were all high as hell but she was acting weird. I started talking to her and she told me who she was on the phone with. I said, "I have beef with that kid and his crew." She said, "I am his connect." I said listen, "I don't care what he said, I am not here for any bullshit." Crystal neglected to inform me that she had called for backup.

The door opened and a black dude came through the door. As he entered, he pulled his hoody up so I could see the gun in his waistband. It was a slick move and it may have scared someone other than me, but what it did with me was make me nervous. Damion leaned in to give Crystal a kiss and in that brief moment his gaze fell onto that girl, my gun was out and the safety was off. I had been shot once and it wasn't going to happen again. Crystal screamed, "No, everything is cool." This was the second time tonight my gun had been drawn. Damion stared straight into my eyes but didn't reach for his gun because I had the drop on him, and from this distance, I couldn't miss. I told Eric, "Take the gun from him." I told Damion, "If you move funny, I will blow your fucking head off." Damion and I would later become friends, but this is how we met.

Eric handed me the gun and I took the bullets out of the .38 Smith and Wesson. I put the bullets in my pocket and tossed the gun on the couch. I said, "I am from New York and I don't know what is going on but I don't like how shit went down." Eric and I left the house, but I had made an impression on Crystal. Crystal got my number and called me when I was back in New York. I invited her to New York and told her she could bring her crew and work. I was trying to impress her so I brought her to all the spots where me and my boys controlled the game.

I didn't know I was playing right into her plan. Crystal would later confide in me that when she first started talking to me, all she had wanted was a door in the New York scene with a dude who had my type of reputation. I liked her because she was the female version of me. Eric was living with me while I was talking to Crystal every day. Damion had come to New York with Crystal and we had become cool. Damion was Crystal's boyfriend, but he knew I wanted her. During this time, I was still messing with Heidi hard and sleeping with many other girls.

The apartment Eric and I lived in Heidi had decorated. Eric and I had been warned about the traffic in and out of our apartment and all the noise. The last straw on us getting kicked out was the day I came home and found Eric butt naked Indian style on the kitchen table surrounded by a circle of empty dust bags, 50 bags of my work. I lost my cool and beat the crap out of Eric until he screamed as if I was killing him. We lost our apartment and I sent Eric back to New Jersey. We were still friends, but we just couldn't live together.

* * * * * *

Now I was living in Brooklyn again. A guy they called Joe Mo was my guy in the neighborhood and he and I had done business for quite a while. Joe was the reason I was accepted in the neighborhood. The guys I bought drugs from in the neighborhood always wanted to move with me, but I had my crew and I wasn't about to let them eat off my plate. I was living with a neighborhood girl, but as usual, I was sleeping with all her friends. The girl I was living with worked at the phone company Bell Atlantic, like many girls in that neighborhood did. My girl and her little friends smoked weed all day long. There was always a bowl full of weed at our apartment. I smoked a lot of dust back then, but I also smoked a lot of bud as well. My girl's friends kept showing up when they knew my girl wasn't home. I know when girls are trying to fuck, so I fucked them.

In the streets, the women who are sleeping with the major drug dealers, are "hands off" because it is a sign of disrespect and can cause a man to lose his life. To have a successful drug business, you must be respected and feared. In the neighborhood I was living in, most of the dealers were bread into the ideologies of mafia rules and most of them thought they were tough. I wasn't from that neighborhood, nor did I fear the mafia so I did what the fuck I wanted. Here I was an outsider getting money in their neighborhood, not putting dudes on, yet I was smashing their chicks. People talk and the girls I was fucking were running their mouths.

I was walking out of my apartment building one morning on my way to get breakfast before heading out to Long Island, when my spider senses started to kick in full gear. I was a drug dealer and a gun fighter and I was always aware of my surroundings. When you are in the streets doing dirt, you have to expect dirt will eventually come back to you. You always need to have a heightened sense of your surroundings, or you will become a victim. In the streets, you are either a predator or prey and I have always chosen the path of predator.

As I was headed towards my truck that was parked in front of my building, I noticed the trap. I saw a guy at the gas station give a sign to a man who was posted up at the bus stop. The man at the bus stop was the shooter, but the bus stop was two buildings away and handguns are intended for close range. Most dudes can't shoot for shit and this was the problem with this idiot. I watched as the shooter grabbed his gun before I could clear my waist and fired, but he missed me. I got a couple shots off in return, but I also wasn't a marksman. I jumped into my truck and attempted to chase the shooter down, but he got away. I was pissed how these pussy ass dudes tried to line me up.

I went on my rounds as usual, but I popped into my old neighborhood and told my childhood boys I was going to line up some robberies for us. In Brooklyn, I was doing business with a lot of guys and I knew their routines. I had a trick for them and I was going to hit them where it hurt, their pockets. I crept back into Brooklyn late at night and called Joe Moe. I met up with Joe and said, "I am about to rob all of the dudes that tried to blast me." Joe said, "I grew up with these dudes, but you are my little man. As far as I am concerned, we never had this conversation." I respected Joe and that's why I told him what I had planned and I understood why he wouldn't go against dudes he knew his whole life. Later in life, he would ask me to kill all his friends, when he found out they were fucking his girl who turned out to be selling pussy.

For the next two days, me and my three-man crew kicked doors in. The first two robberies were easy because I just called and set up my usual deals and backed them down. The Latin King Pundo I made personal and beat him out of his coat, took all his shit, chain, watch, phone, beeper, money and drugs. The other guys I just took their drugs. After Pundo and George, we started to kick doors down. I tricked one dude's girlfriend into opening the door so we could rob them. She was talking big shit yelling, "My man is going to fucking kill you when I tell him you were here" until I reminded her, "You need to be alive to tell him." She gladly gave up everything he had stashed at her house.

Word had spread fast as to what I was up to. The last guy I got wasn't even a major drug dealer or a good take, but with him it was because I didn't like him. The kid sold weed in front of the McDonalds on Coney Island Avenue and after he made the sale, he would hide the money under the payphone. I sat in a car up the block and just watched him. I obviously didn't get everything on my last take because his boss still had work for this idiot. The kid put his work into the pocket of his brand new "Avirex" Jacket and I noticed he didn't give his boss the money from under the phone. Me and my boys got out of the car but I told them to stay back, this would be easy. I pulled my hoody up and pushed the brim of my hat low and put my gun in the front pouch of my hoody. The guy had a couple of people with him but they were all clown so I wasn't worried.

I pushed my way through the crowd until I was in front of this kid. I pulled out the gun and cracked him in the side of his head. When he fell back against the front window of McDonald's, I was up on him going in his pockets. I remember looking over his shoulder and locking eyes with a little girl who was eating a happy meal. I gave the little girl a wink, she didn't know what she was seeing. The kid was crying and said, "Why are you doing me like this? I am not anyone." I just didn't like him because he was a loud mouth and a fake tough guy, but he wasn't tough right now. I looked at him and said, "Take off the jacket now." It was a $500 jacket and he loved it. He acted like he was going to complain until I gave him another love tap with the pistol.

On the way back to the car, I reached under the payphone and took his stash. The last robbery was the only one that was personal. The other guys were all worth the risk. I didn't know who sent the shooter so they would all pay. When I robbed these dealers, I had reasons. I wanted to show them I wasn't playing and I wanted to take over. In order to do this, I had to attempt to put everyone out of business.

My boys were loving me. I took half of everything but I gave them the other half to split amongst themselves and it was a good take. I ended up with two kilos of coke, five pounds of hydroponic weed, five ounces of juice (pcp liquid) 2,000 hits of Ecstasy and money. We also got two guns out of the house, but I let the boys keep them. I was hood rich again. In the drug game, when one drug dealer robs another dealer or in this case, several other dealers, it's like a nice Christmas bonus check. I had the work I had on the streets plus everything I just stole. Some of those guys were my connections at the time, but I'd find new connects. Plus, I had enough work to last a little while with the product I had on the streets. The only downside to this situation was, I now had a whole other group of guys who wanted to kill me. They would all just have to get in line with the rest of my haters.

The difference with this beef and the Limelight crew beef was, the Kings Highway Boys weren't pussy, not all of them anyway. Word on the street was there was money on my head and dudes were popping up places looking for me. I was having plenty of fun with their money and I even lowered my prices to make my crew happy. I showed up at the Club Caffeine that we had on lock down with the drugs and because security was on my payroll, I could always get in with my gun. I was let in the side door as usual and the minute I got inside one of my runners told me there were at least 20 dudes from Brooklyn in the spot armed and looking for me. I had smoked so much dust that I felt like King Kong and was talking some wild west gunslinger shit to my boy, but he convinced me to leave with him. We took a couple of girls with us and went to the hotel that was up the block from the club. We partied in the room with the girls until I passed out. I had smoked so much dust I couldn't even fuck. In a drug induced fog, I just watched the girls break off with each other until I fell out.

* * * * * *

I couldn't move around because these guys were popping up everywhere looking for me. I needed to get out of New York for a little while. I collected the money that was owed to me and went to see Matt and my crew. I hit them off with some drugs and told them I was going to Philly for a while. I saw Heidi and my people over around her way and did the same. I left my car in my old neighborhood and got on the bus heading to Philly. I called Crystal on my cell phone and told her I was on my way. New York knew I robbed the Kings Highway boys, but Philly was a world away. I showed up at Crystals with a Backpack and duffle bag. The bags were loaded with drugs, money, my jewelry and two guns. I could buy new clothes and whatever else I needed.

When I got to Crystal's house I didn't take the bags off or tell her anything other than to call Damion and tell him I was coming over. I was acting weird but Crystal had been talking to me long enough to know I was weird. Damion and I had become cool after our first run-in when he came to NY with Crystal. Money and a steady flow of drugs had the ability to mend fences. Damion was a partner in a record shop and label called "911 Records" but he was knee deep in the Philly drug game. Damion was the brains but his brother Dom was the muscle. Dom had just come home from a state bid for attempted murder. Crystal told me Damion was waiting for me so I went to Damion's house and he let me in. I had been there enough times I knew where his room was so I headed up the stairs and walked in his room. Once Damion came in I shut the door and locked it. Damion looked at me strange, but he sat on his bed and watched as I opened the duffle bag and started pulling out drugs. It was more impressive to show than tell. With a nice catch of drugs sitting on his carpet, I told him, "Let's get money", I explained what was going on and that I was going to lay up in Philly for a minute. In Philly, they had dirt weed and coke was more expensive. I had exotic weed and plenty of coke. I needed Damion's connections to move the work and I would give him enough room to make money.

We were working out the game plan when Crystal called. I could hear she was excited and not in a good way. Damion gave me the phone and Crystal was explaining how two kids from Brooklyn had just pushed their way into her house saying they were looking for me. She told them I wasn't there and Kendrick her roommate from Baltimore, had gotten them out of the house. She wanted to know what was going on. I didn't know how they found me or knew about Crystal, but someone had given me up. What the fuck was I going to do now?

I told Crystal to find some place for us to go and I would explain everything later. I told her to call a car service and when she left, to take a ride around the block and make sure no one was following her. Once she knew no one was following her call on the cell phone and I would come out and we would leave. Crystal was a rider. She knew how to handle the drug business and if need be, she knew how to handle the guns. She found us a place to go and followed my directions. I got into the car and we went to her girlfriend's house who lived in the suburbs outside of the city. In the car, she didn't ask me anything because she knew better than to talk in front of the driver.

When we arrived, Crystal's girlfriend let us in. When the girlfriend shut the door, I locked the door and looked around the apartment, closed the blinds and pulled the two bags off and put them on the floor in the living room. I told Crystal to open the bags and look inside. Crystal and her girlfriend's eyes almost popped out of their heads when they saw the contents of my bags. I told Crystal and her friend the story, only leaving out the part about all the girls I was sleeping with.

Crystal and I stayed at her girlfriend's house for a week. I took the girls shopping and out to eat. Crystal and I shared a bed and we started having sex. Late one night she revealed the truth about her intentions with me in the past, but now things were different and she had fallen for me. Crystal told me she wanted me to move in with her. No one else had shown up looking for me, so we went back to the townhouse. This is how I ended up living in Philly. When I ended up stealing Crystal from Damion, he bowed out for the sake of being able to get into the New York drug loop.

EIGHT

WELCOME TO THE 215

"Somewhere deep down there's a decent man in me, he just can't be found." -Eminem

The townhouse in Philly was a modern style design. When you came through the front door you would be in the living room. The stairs to the house were spiral. From the living room, you could see into the kitchen that had sliding glass doors which led out to a small enclosed yard. Under the kitchen, was a small room that Howie lived in and the laundry room. Our bedroom was up the stairs from the living room and it had a big bay window that overlooked the yard. The floor above our bedroom was Justin's bedroom and bathroom then a few more stairs led you to an area that Kendrick and Justin used as their DJ area. Kendrick's bedroom and bathroom were located on the top floor and overlooked the DJ/audio studio. Howie was born and raised in Philly, Justin was from Allentown PA and Kendrick was from Baltimore. Crystal had grown up right outside of Philly and I was from New York. Everyone in the house sold drugs and had their own business where they were from. We weren't hand to handing drugs out of the house, but we all ended up working together.

Philly's rave scene was small but it was growing. I wandered into a club called "Fever" and when I got into the club there wasn't anyone in the spot but the owner and his staff. The owner was a mob guy, and the club ran an under the table casino twice a month, so he kept the club open every night. It made things easier when it came to explaining the money. I approached the owner and gave him my sales pitch. I lied about my experience throwing parties because at this point, I had never thrown a rave of my own, but I had been around the top guys in New York while they put everything together.

I walked out of that club with an agreement I could have Thursday nights. I brought Damion and my roommates in on the deal. I was just looking for another place I could control the drug trade. The club took off and it worked out for everyone involved. Thursdays worked out well for me because I would sneak back into New York for Friday, Saturday and Sunday because even though there were dudes trying to kill me, I still needed to attend to my business.

I still had beef with the Limelight crew and the Kings Highway boys, but I had my own crew and we were strong. When I went out to the raves, I would bring my usual runners as well as my goons. Dudes in the hood always wanted to come out and fuck freaky raver chicks and in the rave drug game, there was never a shortage of this. My problem with chasing tail would later fuck everything up.

Crystal and I were doing well. Crystal worked at the hottest clothing store on South Street so I was always fly. During this time, I was in the club and all eyes were on me. I looked like a Tommy Hilfiger/Polo poster boy with a ghetto twist. I was up on the brands and I had items before everyone else had them. The girls loved me before and now they really loved me.

I should have been happy with everything I had, but I wasn't. With me something was always missing. I had a main girlfriend and her father was loading me up with work, me and my roommates were working together making money up and down the top of the East coast and the safe was always nice and full. I was just 18 years old and had more than most 40-year old's. But as a young man, I wanted it all and the freedom of having money at such a young age, made me feel like I could get away with anything.

I would leave Philly, get into New York where I had a Spanish girl name Mariel. Mariel wasn't a club girl and it seemed like she was related to half of the building she lived in. There wasn't anyone stupid enough to try and go up in that building and steal my stash. Mariel was good because she followed directions to the letter when it came to taking care of my business interests when I wasn't around, plus she loved to fuck. The only problem was, she had the Latina temper. She knew I had other girls but as long as I took care of her, she was cool.

After I would leave the City I would head to Long Island where I had Heidi. I would stay at Heidi's parents' house with her where I had a safe. Heidi had been with me long enough that she could deal with everyone. Heidi and I would sleep with each other from the time we met until I would be carted off to prison. Heidi and I hated each other, but we had amazing sex. She couldn't say no to me and I wouldn't say no to her.

The truth of the matter is, I wasn't ever very good unless I had a woman in my corner to try to keep me focused. I was good at making money, but I couldn't hold it unless my women were taking it away from me. If I didn't have a woman to keep me on schedule, I would blow shit off and hang out and get high. I didn't learn how to do laundry until I came to prison because I always had women doing my laundry or I would just buy new clothes. Because I was so selfish I hurt all the women in my life and they all loved me but I wasn't capable of loving anyone. I didn't think I could ever love a woman, but one day I would fall in love.

At the time, I was running from Philly to New York and I felt like it was my god given right to do whatever I felt like. I was so bold, I brought Crystal with me telling her these girls were just part of my business and nothing else. The girls knew Crystal was my main chick and they knew her father was one of my connects, so they played along to keep me happy. For a little while, I had it all and it was working out for me. I was so confident in myself, I started slipping on other precautions I used to take. Dennis the Menace, Frankie Bones and his crew threw another big party at the Brooklyn Armory. I had beef with the guys Dennis and Frankie grew up with, but I was always cool with them, plus they were getting too much legal money to care about petty street beef. I showed up to the party with a car full of girls and an artist kid named Zane. Zane later would do comics for "Heavy Metal Magazine". Zane was a cool raver kid and a nasty graffiti artist, but he wasn't a gangster.

On the way into the Rave I met two guys from Florida. I took a liking to these two guys and since they were part of the Florida scene, I wanted to show them some New York hospitality. I would get lucky once again, on a fluke I met these two not knowing they were the biggest Ecstasy dealers in Florida. Chris was Latino, from Miami and Ethan was Asian and white from Fort Myers. They were in New York because things got crazy for them in Florida. Chris's uncle owned the apartment in Harlem they were staying in. I was on the VIP list so I got everyone in.

The Armory was packed just like the last party Dennis had thrown. Once again, the DJ's were upstairs with everyone who was someone. The pawn laser operator was a friend of ours from the Philly scene. Pawn lasers are the same lasers from the "Pink Floyd laser light show". The guy who created the lasers was from Texas but he had companies in a few major cities. As usual, I was smoking dust and I was sharing with everyone and my new friends. My new friends could tell I was in the loop, so we exchanged numbers and they told me they could do good numbers for me.

The girls and Zane were downstairs dancing and running around while Crystal and I spent half of the night upstairs talking business with Dennis and the A-listers. I was trying to line up some of the New York DJ's to come to Fever now that the club was taking off. I hadn't brought any of my workers or goons with me and I had left the gun in

Megan's Caravan that was parked around the corner. Crystal and I decided to go downstairs and see what was going on so I told Chris and Ethan we'd seen them later. I had already introduced them to everyone, and they were having fun with the Royal Court.

Crystal and I had both been smoking a lot of dust. I was holding Crystals hand as we navigated through the sea of bodies. It was about 3am and the rave was really going strong. Crystal and I turned the corner and came face to face with the Latin King Pundo who was the Kings Highway boy that I robbed for all the juice and beat the shit out of, on the first day of my Brooklyn robbery spree. Pundo was with a bunch of his boys and seeing him sobered me up really quick. He said, "Let's see if you make it out of here alive." I bluffed and put my hand under my shirt and said, "What do you think, the gun that you have was the last one that came off the production line? I don't go nowhere without my hammer and I will leave your bitch ass stinking right here."

Crystal stood at my side lost and confused until I pulled her on our getaway path. It was time to get out of this spot. We needed to find the girls and Zane as fast as possible. It took us awhile to round everyone up, but we finally found everyone and made our exit out of a side door. I just needed to get to my gun and I'd be alright. The snow had started coming down and we were moving towards the minivan when I heard my name. I told Crystal and the rest of them to go and I turned around and tried my bluff again. This time it wouldn't work and I saw Pundo draw his gun as if it was happening in slow motion. I started to run as the sounds of the shots erupted and made it to the minivan without being shot. I got the gun and the little girl Megan drove around the corner to see if we could find them now that I was armed, and the odds were now equal. Megan was a little white girl with glasses, blonde hair and freckle but her little ass carried a gravity knife and was down for whatever. Megan had more heart than Zane. We didn't see Pundo so we headed back to Philly.

The next day Chris and Ethan called me and I invited them down to Philly. They showed up and after that we would spend the next couple of years as partners. Chris and Ethan's crew in Florida were running the show while they were with me and they could get drugs sent through the mail to wherever they told their guys to send them. The Ecstasy they were getting me was much cheaper than the pills in New York. The quality of the pills wasn't as good, but the pills still moved.

The only problem was, Chris was a psycho. Chris slept with a shotgun and he believed the FBI was following him and he would sketch out. Chris was a killer and the things he had been through made him crazy. Ethan was the complete opposite, he was laid back and a people person. This was now my crew and we were always together. Sometimes Ethan would stay back and chill out but for all business, Chris was with me because no one ever played around with Chris. Even if you didn't know him, you could sense he was dangerous. The only time Chris wasn't crazy intense is when he was dancing. Chris was a break dancer and I mean a "stop the crowd and watch in awe when he hit the battle circle in any club", break dancer. Chris's craziness came in handy in my business though.

* * * * * *

I had started selling cheap pounds of weed to a few of the young kids who lived in the projects who were on the block over from us. My roommates told me to leave that shit alone. I didn't need the little bit of money this particular business venture brought me and the business was too close to home. None of us needed the heat, plus the older guys from the projects wouldn't appreciate me cutting their throats with my cheap prices. My roommates reasoning was sound, but I did whatever I felt like anyway. I kept the quarter pounds and ounces at Damion's house because when I wasn't in Philly, Damion could take care of business.

The older dudes from the projects had figured the set up out and they were pissed. They sent a few young kids down the block where I happened to be outside talking on my cell phone. The kids told me they needed a quarter pound. I called Damion and told him I was coming around the block. When you got to the end of the block, you could either go right and this would lead you to the side of the projects, or go left past the abandoned building. Past the abandoned building if you made a right there was a half block and this was where Damion and Dom's house was. South Philly has a lot of small little blocks. I trooped down the block with the two young black kids as I had done a bunch of times in the past. The only difference about this journey was, these kids had been squeezed by the older guys to set me up. They weren't trying to rob me, but they were about to send me a message how they didn't appreciate me selling drugs in their hood.

When I turned the corner, and approached the front of the abandoned building, the two kids ran off and out of the shadows emerged about ten dudes from the projects. I didn't have a gun on me but I could fight and fight I did. They made sure I didn't make it back onto my block so we fought the long way around the block. I would fight, they would jump me and I'd get loose and make some forward ground and get jumped again. I made it back to the townhouse after I got jumped about ten times or so.

They had beaten me pretty good, but they didn't get my money, my cellphone, or my jewelry. The only thing I lost was my beeper which had slid off at some point. I walked into the house and Crystal's screams brought everyone in the house to the living room. The First Down vest I had on was covered in blood and my face looked like Martins in the episode of his show where he fought the boxer "Tommy the Hitman Herns". Blood was coming out of my mouth and nose, I was bruised up pretty good and I was pissed. I was ranting and raving about as soon as night fell, we were going into the projects and we were going to kill these guys. The problem was, I was all by myself because all I was getting from my roommates was a lot of "I told you to leave the projects alone and you're going to bring heat to the house." I couldn't believe what I was hearing because had it been anyone of them, I would have been ready to ride on whoever.

I went and got my beat-up body in the tub and soaked, got really drunk and fell asleep. I woke up really early and called a car service and got on the Peter Pan bus to New York. I didn't drive back and forth from Philly and New York because it was safer to transport drugs on the bus. Once I arrived in New York, I took a cab to Harlem. Chris and Ethan were with his uncle. They had just arrived from Florida and they had brought a bunch of Kilo's, plus Ecstasy for me. I walked into the apartment and Chris took one look at my face and you could see the crazy man coming to the surface. This is what I had banked on.

Chris and Ethan's Chevy Beretta had a huge stash box they used to transport drugs. We decided to load the stash box with guns. Chris's favorite gun was a twelve-gauge shotgun with a pistol grip on it. The twelve gauge was the gun he slept with and the reason everyone was very careful when it was time to wake him up. Chris was formulating the game plan as we drove back to Philly. As swollen and stiff as I was, I was also excited because revenge was in my grasp.

When we got back to Philly we found a parking spot on the block and unloaded all our arsenal. My roommates were not happy to see who I brought home, as if they didn't know when they woke up and found me gone what I was up to. I guess they were just hoping I would let this go. I was 18 years old and thought I was gangster. There was no way I was going to let the beating I took be the end of this. We had our game plan. Ethan knew what the plan was but our plan would only require Chris and me. I didn't let Crystal or my roommates know what we were planning to do, but they knew something was going to happen and everyone in the house kept voicing reasonable suggestions of non-action. We pretended to listen and played video games and smoked weed until we passed out.

Chris woke me up before anyone in the house was awake and we put our plan into action. Looking back on this now, it is a miracle we didn't get arrested for this, but this is what we did. I put two 9mm's into my waistband and went into the street. Chris had loaded the shotgun with two bird shots, one slug, another bird shot and the last slug. Bird shot sprays BB's and the further away you are the more BB's spread out. I was in the street screaming bullshit trying to get the project kids to come around the corner from where they sold drugs. The more I ranted, guys started coming around the corner but they weren't coming up the block. Chris was standing in my doorway with the shotgun where he couldn't be seen. The project boys were coming around the corner to see what the crazy white boy was yelling about. When a nice enough group was standing on the corner I pulled the two handguns out and started firing in the direction of the crowd. Chris came out of the doorway and let off one shot, then another shot and finally a third shot. What we didn't know was, the handle of the shotgun had cracked and when the slug fired, the shotgun broke clear and ended up in the living room wall.

I don't know if we hit anyone, but I felt better about getting my ass kicked. We ran back into the house, not a very smart move, but this is what we did. My roommates were going crazy and flipping out. Ethan had gotten up and was making breakfast for himself as if nothing had happened. Crystal was crying and Chris started wigging out so he and I left the house, got into the car and went to North Philly.

* * * * * *

I was doing dust business with the guys on Dolphin. I would bring them ounces of juice and they would cut it and make their bundles. They cut the dust more than we would ever dare to in New York, but it still gave them better dust than the other blocks sold. I had met the guys at my club Fever. North Philly and South Philly don't usually get along, so the boys loved to hear we were terrorizing the boys in the projects. Chris and I hung out in North Philly all day smoking dust, drinking bootleg liquor that came in 40oz bottles and was fluorescent green with a skull on the label, and watched the boys make sales. It was time to go back to the house because we had left Ethan and I needed to make sure my roommates were ok. We didn't have the shotgun because it broke, but I had brought the two handguns, reloaded them and we headed back home.

The kids in the projects served drug addicts on the side of their building that was closest to my block. This was the same side they jumped me on that day. The dealers knocked out all the lights so they could avoid the cops while hustling. They called that side of the building "The Darkside". Chris and I decided we would give the boys one more go. The Darkside block was one way and lead to Washington Street and that was good for us because once we hit Washington we could make a right and be back on Randolph, which was my block. The problem was, the projects were on the driver's side and I was to be the shooter while Chris drove.

I knew how the guys made sales, the cars would flick their lights and dudes would come out of hiding and serve whoever. I climbed onto the window and sat on the frame leaning over the roof with the gun pointed in the darkness. Chris flicked the lights and I saw movement in the dark and I just kept hitting the trigger until the clip was empty. I was basically shooting into the darkness but you can bet the project boys were running for cover. I climbed back into my seat and we were out of there. We hit two rights and parked and walked towards the house. When we got into the house Crystal was pissed but happy to see me. I went to our room and said, "I had to do something or I wouldn't be able to look at myself in the mirror. I am not playing gangster anymore, this is my life." I explained to her, "if I'm going to die, it will be on my feet not my knees."

The good thing about Philly is people mind their business. All that drama and shooting and I never saw a cop car come around. When we got up, Chris, Ethan and I packed up the car and came back to New York. Crystal went to her father's house because I didn't want her in the house due to the beef. When I called to check on my roommates, Justin and his friend from Allentown had gotten jumped when they went to the corner store, because the project boys were jumping any white dudes they caught in the neighborhood. I told my roommate he shouldn't have acted like a bitch right after it happened. I really didn't feel bad because they didn't want to help me when I got jumped. The shit eventually died down, but I didn't come out of the house without my gun ready. It seemed like everywhere I went, someone wanted to kill me and by this point, I was used to it.

Besides the drama I had in my life, things were good for me. Fever was doing well on my night and the owner Dominic took a liking to me after I started bringing in all that money. One night, a guy was giving Dominic and his security problems so I jumped in. Dominic was sleeping with the bartender and everyone in the club staff knew it. One of the customers had grabbed her and Dominic and his bouncer grabbed the guy and tried to throw him out. This guy swung on Dominic so I cracked him in the head with a bottle, and he went down. Dominic and the bouncer dragged the guy up the stairs and left him in the street. Dominic pulled me into the office and was yelling, "Jeff, I can get sued!" I said, "He was swinging on you so I cracked him." Dominic was a street guy and loyalty was important to him. After that, he treated me like I was his son.

Thursday nights were rave nights at Fever, but Saturday nights, Fever hosted a hip-hop night. Usually, I would be in NY on Fridays, but because I was a fan of the late and great BIG I decided to go to the club. I got there early so I could help Dominic set up and after Biggie and Junior Mafia did their sound check, we all went to the back room to smoke a couple of blunts and talk about Brooklyn. It's funny, in my experiences those who we perceive to be superstars are just regular people like us.

* * * * * *

One day when I was coming home from New York, I ran into Tom from Long Island and he was going to Philly to stay with some raver chick he was dealing with. I used to see Tom at raves and different clubs but he didn't work for me anymore, so I wouldn't see him very often. However, our bond was still strong. We got onto the Peter Pan bus after we got beer for the ride. I had a lot of money on me because I was going home. On the bus, we decided to pop some really good Ecstasy and I was moving. By the time we got to Philly, we were both feeling really good. I convinced Tom to come back to the house to hang out and I said his girl could come back to my house too and then we could all go out. There was a lot of traffic so Tom and I got out of the cab and cut through the back block where the abandoned building was at.

We came onto my block and there were three young black guys from the projects hanging out. As we passed them the leader of the pack said, "Can I get a dollar?" Tom and I were both street kids from New York and we knew the setup for a robbery when we saw it. I had my money in a leather carry case that had my phone numbers as well as the ID I had in the gypsy Eric's name. The window to the townhouse was open and I wasn't about to get robbed for all that money by the three stooges so I threw the case through the window. By the time I turned around, Tom had a knife out and was poking our would-be robbers. The guys ran off and Tom and I slipped into the house. Kendrick and Crystal were in the living room when we came in and we explained what just happened. You need to remember, the cops hadn't showed up after all the shootings, but somehow, they showed up for this.

Crystal and Kendrick were outside talking to the police but I had warrants in New York and I wasn't trying to go outside. Tom and I were inside safe until Crystal came in the house and said, "The cops just want to talk to you guys. They said they're not going to lock you up." I said, "If we go out there, we are going to get arrested!" Crystal said, "We have too much shit in this house so if the cops come in, we are all going to jail." Tom and I ended up going outside to see what was going on and the minute we stepped out of the house, we were cuffed and thrown into the back of the cop car. Mind you, the Ecstasy was flowing through our systems at full speed about this time. I had warrants out for my arrest in NY and the ID I had said my name was Eric Dukes. I needed Tom to remember this so I kept drilling the name into his head on our ride. The officers took us to the hospital where the kid who was cooperating was able to ID us. The kid said, "That's them, but my friend was trying to rob them." This statement saved us.

The cops uncuffed us and said, "We just need a statement from you two." I said, "I am drunk so I don't know what happened." Tom started with his story but the problem was, his story started on a bus with his friend Jeff. I'm sitting there thinking if they print me or figure out who I am, I am going to jail until I get extradited back to New York. The cop left the desk for a minute and I looked at Tom and said, "My name is Eric." Thankfully he remembered and the second half of his story was him and Eric. Somehow, we got out of the precinct and even got a ride home because the cops were worried the project boys were going to kill us. How funny is that after the drama I really had with those guys?

The next day Tom goes to the girls house he was supposed to meet and I go back to New York. A couple days later, Crystal called me and told me the cops were looking for us but she told them she didn't know us. Thank god for lazy cops and Commonwealth laws. In New York, we would have gotten locked up, but in PA you have self-defense laws.

* * * * * *

Chris and Ethan were coming back and forth from Florida and when they got up North, they would meet up with me and we would pop up all over the place. We would go to Baltimore and Virginia with Kendrick and his crew. There was a Rave club called the Freight Yard in Allentown that Justin used to DJ at and we would go there and sell drugs. New York was home base for me and we were always there. We had a guy in Massachusetts named Ziggy. The cops couldn't build cases on us because we didn't stick around for more than a day or two. The only guys who knew how to get in touch with us, were guys in our inner circle.

With Chris I was good because he was so paranoid, no one would ever catch me slipping. One day I was on Kings Highway with Chris, and Pundo found out I was in the neighborhood because I was being reckless and fucking with the young kids and some girls. A kid who worked for Pundo told him and we got into a shootout right on Avenue V, but Chris's paranoia is why I am not dead. Chris saw the Pathfinder and put me on to what was about to go down. I was able to drop the seat before the bullets ripped through the window, and Chris had gotten out of the car and fired which made them pull off. If not for him, I'd be dead.

I had to pay to have Chris's car fixed and hear his mouth as we drove back to Philly with no side windows, but at least I was alive. When they shot the passenger side windows they were trying to hit me but the tints caused my window to fold in and the driver's side to blow out, even though the door was ajar when Chris rolled out of the car. The whole situation was out of control, but I wasn't as shaken up as the two girls that were from the neighborhood and in the backseat of the car when this all happened.

At this point in my life, I believed I was going to die. My life was filled with so much gun play, it became almost normal to me. I slept with a gun under my pillow and if you saw me, you could bet I had a gun on me or nearby. Looking back on my life, I am truly lucky to have been only hit once and still be alive. My mother told me I wouldn't live to see 21 years old and here I am, writing this story at 40. For some reason, I am still alive.

NINE

WOMEN SCORNED

"Hell hath no fury like a woman scorned" - William
Congreve

I was making my runs back and forth from Philly to New York and
back again. I was playing house with three different women and I
thought I could go on like this forever, but a woman scorned will always
be a stupid man's downfall and I was a stupid man.

I came back to Mariel's apartment after being awake for more than
24 hours and on way too many drugs. I was trying to go to sleep and
Mariel wanted to fuck, but I just didn't have the energy. The fact I
didn't want to do what she wanted me to do started a fight. She said,
"Why don't you take your ass back to your white bitch?" All I wanted to
do was sleep, but I knew I wasn't going to sleep here so I got up and
said, "Fine, I think I'll do that." I trooped my tired ass into Manhattan
and caught the next bus to Philly.

I was catching a bunch of 666 beeps from Mariel, but I shut the
pager off and caught a little sleep on the bus. I didn't know Mariel was
so mad I wouldn't return her calls, that she decided to called Crystal. I
was really in trouble now. Mariel told Crystal how she was my girl and

had been for years and every night I ate her pussy and fucked her. As if this wasn't enough, she told Crystal I was only with her because her father was my connect. I was in a world of trouble and all I wanted to do was go to sleep. I had no clue for the hurricane I was caught in.

I came into the house and put all the money in our safe. I kept a twenty-dollar bill because I was going to go to the corner store to get cigarettes and something to eat before I slept. By the time I came up the stairs, Crystal was on me and she was going nuts repeating everything Mariel told her. I thought quickly and said, "She is fucking lying because she is pissed off I didn't give her money." Crystal wasn't going for my bullshit and I was tired so I said, "We can talk about this later, I just need to fucking sleep!" I walked out the front door as this crazy woman was cursing me out. I heard the door open, but I knew it was Crystal and I figured she was just going to follow me down the street and continue to yell so I didn't bother turning around to look. I had bought Crystal a little chrome .25 with a pearl handle for her protection. Crystal let off three shots at me and I ran until I hit the corner.

I had people all over the place trying to kill me and now my girlfriend was one of them. I was tired and pissed off. I couldn't go home and I didn't have enough money for a hotel. I ended up going to the arcade on South Street and sat in the "drive in" game and rested. I ran into some of the guys I knew and when I told them what happened, they told me I was stupid because Crystal was the best catch in Philly. All I knew was, I still wanted to kill her right at that moment.

I linked up with Zane and we went to the club. Dominic gave me a few dollars and let me catch two hours of sleep in the office. Dominic was like a father to me and he told me not to do anything stupid. Zane and I caught a taxi and went back to the house at around 2am. Before I went into the house, Zane said, "Don't do anything crazy." We walked in and Kendrick's two friends were sitting on the couch smoking weed. Zane sat down with the guys and I went upstairs and quietly opened our door.

Our bed had a red velvet blanket with black satin sheets and Crystal had fallen asleep on top of the covers. She had a pair of little lace undies that were creeping up her ass and a t-shirt on. Her strawberry blonde hair laid in wavy curls across the pillow. She looked beautiful as she slept. I stared at her for a minute and then slapped the hell out of her to awake her from her slumber. She awoke screaming as I grabbed her by her feet and dragged her out of the bed and down the stairs. Everyone in the living room was in shock as I continued to drag her by her feet into the kitchen. In the kitchen, I was screaming, "Everyone is trying to kill me and now you are trying to kill me over some lying bitch?" Kendrick's friends tackled me and broke us up. Crystal was crying and I knew I was fucked up for putting my hands on her. The drugs and the pressures of my life had made me snap. We made up and spent the next three days together where I promised I wouldn't stay at any of the girls houses while I was in New York. I was lying, but I didn't want to lose Crystal.

I had to go to New York and deal with Mariel though. Mariel had almost fucked everything up and she knew better. The problem was, Mariel was a hood chick and she wasn't soft. She had grown up in the biggest projects in New York Queensbridge. I got to the building and hit the buzzer. I didn't have my keys because I had thrown them when I was leaving during our last fight.

Mariel answered the intercom and said, "Papi I was mad and I am sorry, but I am not letting you in because you seem very mad at me." She wasn't letting me in because she knew I was going to lose it. An old woman was leaving the building and I caught the door and went upstairs to the apartment. Mariel answered the door with the chain lock on and said, "Promise me you are not going to act up if I let you in." I said, "I'm not promising shit, open the fucking door." Mariel and I had fought like cats and dogs before and she could hold her own. She knew me and knew how I was.

When she finally opened the door, I tried to swing on her but she was already getting out of the way. The main hallway led into the kitchen and I chased her into the kitchen, but to my surprise, she had grabbed a huge knife out of the chopping block and was now trying to stab me. My offense had now become defense and she was chasing me around with this big knife. I got out of the apartment and away. Mariel's aunt came and found me and played peacemaker and we made up.

In less than a week, two girls had come closer to killing me then all the guys who were trying to do me in. I was a crazy kid and the women in my life were just as crazy. Heidi was the only one of them who wasn't violent. My girls may try to kill me, but what they wouldn't do was call the cops on me and I was alright with this. I thought I was so slick but I wasn't. Crystal was just letting me dig my own grave. I was back to my routine as usual.

About a month later I showed up at Heidi's house and let myself in. I went down to Heidi's room and to my surprise, Crystal was sitting on the waterbed with Heidi who had this stupid look on her face when I opened the door. Crystal said, "What the hell are you doing here?" She didn't even wait for a response and she went on saying, "I can't believe you are cheating on me! I don't have men cheat on me, and with this?" I couldn't believe she said that right in front of Heidi, like she wasn't even there. Heidi was cute, but Crystal was a show stopper. Crystal said, "You have a choice, you can come home with me and we will work it out, but you can't come back to New York anymore." I started talking big shit and said, "Go fuck yourself, I choose New York." Crystal said, "I took all the money out of the safe and brought it to my father's house." Crystal was much smarter than I was and she had played her hand very well. Very calmly, Crystal got up, called a car service and left. Crystal hadn't gone to Mariel's because she may have been tough, but that shit wouldn't have worked with Mariel. Mariel and her girls would have drug her ass around the projects. But Crystal was smart and she had all the money. I let my pride and stupidity cause me to lose all my money.

I had product on the streets and I still had Chris and Ethan but I lost my Crystal meth connection and the deals with my roommates. As had become my MO, I put a team together and we robbed everyone but Crystal's father and Damion. The Philly boys put $50,000 on my head, but no one would be stupid enough to try.

I was back in New York full time and I was smoking enough dust to fill two dead bodies with embalming fluid. I felt as though I owed Dominic a goodbye, because he had become like a father figure to me. I showed up at Fever and went into the office. I explained to him everything that transpired and I told him I wouldn't be in Philly anymore, but they could keep Fever going. He wanted me to stay, but I had already robbed everyone so I felt like it was time to go back to New York permanently.

Bullshit Billy was from Patchogue and a member of the AU (Abstract Universal) crew. I convinced his female roommate it would be best if she moved out because we were about to use that apartment as home base. The apartment gave my runners a place to stay, even if they had to sleep on the floor. I stayed with Heidi or Mariel most of the time, but it wasn't like going home to Philly where I used to be able to rest and get my mind together. Crystal had been a big part of keeping me focused and now I didn't have that. One night I called Crystal in a PCP stupor and begged her to let me come home. She laughed at me and told me I no longer had a home. Crystal was the one who told me there was money on my head. My nice life in Philly had come to an end. It was back to the mean streets of the Big Apple all day every day.

TEN

SPIRALING OUT OF CONTROL

"Addiction is the only prison where the locks are on the inside" -Unknown

I got lucky once again. Before Crystal had kicked me out, Chris, Crystal and one of her girlfriends and I went to a big rave in Massachusetts. The ride up there was hell and took forever because Chris was catching his paranoid attacks about the FBI following us, so the trip involved a lot of hitting random exits and getting lost. This was all before GPS. The fact that in the car with us was a half of a kilo of cocaine and a book of LSD, had Crystal and her girlfriend scared. I was used to it at this point.

The drugs we had were for the guy who was throwing the rave, but we were supposed to be in Massachusetts hours before the party and arrive with him. But now the party was underway and we arrived late because of the lunatic. We showed up with the girls crying and when we got to the door, there was a problem with the list. Chris punched the guy in the face and pushed his way in. It would have gotten worse if the guy who was throwing the party hadn't made it to the door to straighten things out. We got in and before the after party, we handled business.

The after party was in some sort of army base building and Chris was now convinced the guy who we sold the drugs to was a rat, and the minute everyone got inside, we were going to be arrested. Chris's reasoning's sometimes were so clear that his conspiracies seemed real, but I told him if the FBI was going to get us, they would have got us once we handed off the drugs.

I finally got everyone to go inside and Chris started break dancing. As usual, it drew a crowd. An older dude started talking to me and said he was from the West Coast. He had been looking for someone to deal with on the East Coast so we exchanged numbers and that was the end of it. I used to meet all sorts of people who would tell me they could do everything under the sun. It just came with the business. I had my sky pager number on the business cards I would give out. Most of the time I didn't remember the people when they called. I had a horrible drug habit.

* * * * * *

I was back in New York and bought myself a new Mazda RX-7 because I no longer had Crystal as my voice of reason about my spending. Robbing Crystals friends didn't cover what I lost from her taking all the money, and I had lost business due to our breakup. I was spending more than I was making. I was about to sabotage myself when I got a page from an LA area code. I call and the guy on the other end had to refresh my memory of who he was. He was smart enough not to talk on the phone about business, but he asked me for an address and told me he wanted me to look at a game he created. I gave him Heidi's address and that was the end of the call.

A couple days later Heidi told me a package came for me. I shot over to the house and when we opened the packaged there was a sealed Monopoly game as if it came from the store. The only difference was, the box was heavier than it should have been. I opened the game and there was a pound of Crystal meth and a card that said, "Call Scooter from a clean line and phone number." The meth Crystal and I were selling before was crank or what they called bathtub meth. The color was either piss yellow or dirty gray. The Crystal Scooter sent was almost clear with a slight pink tint. I ended up calling it; "Pink Shaboo Glass" as a marketing strategy. I called Scooter right away. Scooter told me really simple, "You can take that pound and run off. I'm in Cali, I won't chase you or you can send me $7500 and we can do business." Crystal and I had been selling the crank for $1000 an ounce and only making $200 off each one. This meth was twice as good and at $7500 a pound this meant each ounce was costing me a little over $450. With the new connect and because the quality of the product was much better, I was able to cut it which allowed me to produce a larger profit. I was now tripling my profit, opposed to making a little off each sale. Plus, this guy sent the drugs first so I didn't have to lay out any money. I wasn't about to fuck this up.

I went to the Western Union and pushed Scooter the money out of my own stash that was dwindling down but I needed this guy to see I was about money. Since I didn't have to rush to get the money right away, I took two ounces and bagged them up in $20 bags so my runners could hit the clubs and spread the word. Since I had gotten the work so cheap, I made the bags bigger than usual and gave my workers great deals. Everyone was happy.

My LSD connection was a hit and miss but I had Ecstasy whenever I needed it through Chris and my other connections. Scooter once a month would cook up a batch for me. The best part about Chris and Scooter was, with them I didn't need money in hand. They trusted me to get them their money.

* * * * * *

I was hanging out with Nancy who was Dennis's ex-girlfriend when I met a girl named Autumn. Nancy and I were sleeping together at this time and we were hanging out with her friends when they decided they wanted to go clubbing. Nancy was still in the loop and all the girls at the house looked good, but I needed to buy an outfit. I had shown up at the house on my motorcycle and had been getting fucked up the whole time. Autumn told me she would drive me to the mall. Autumn was a smart college girl who had a 4.0 GPA at Hofstra. This girl spoke like eight different languages, and I'm talking like she is beefing with the Chinese grocer rapid fire. We spent a couple of weeks hanging out and I still hadn't slept with her. This is something that never happened. At my best, I may have hung out for a night or two without sex, but too many girls were willing to fuck me.

I eventually started living with Autumn, and around this time, I started using Heroin. My drug habit was so out of control, prior to this, I was chasing a high I could never reach. I had sold dope several times in the past and tried it, but I didn't really like it. Back then it was too intense, but at this point in my life I was searching for intense and I found it in a bag of Heroin.

I was making so much money selling drugs, I didn't think of myself as a junky. I had a nice car, a nice motorcycle, we lived in a nice house and I wore the hottest fashions. I was not someone people perceived as a junky. A junky is someone who is broke, often homeless and people tend to have sympathy for junkies. When a junky steals food from the local grocery store, it is usually because he is starving. I on the other hand, had an endless supply of money and drugs. The truth was, I was worse off than most of the drug addicts living in the streets, I was just better at hiding it.

* * * * * *

In the club scene, Special K was becoming big. Special K is Ketamine. Ketamine is a small animal tranquilizer. The bottles came in 10ml bottles and a case was 144 bottles. Each bottle made 12-14 $20 bags. I couldn't get enough bottles so I started robbing the kids who were selling the cases. I met the one kid when we were in the audience of the "Ricki Lake Show". I was hanging out at the FIT campus as I had for years, and the show was giving out tickets on the campus. This all happened when Autumn and I were still just hanging out. The kid kept setting up deals, but he would only come up with 12 or 24 bottles. I bought them because I wanted to make the robbery worth my while. Ivan who was my childhood friend and stick up partner kept coming into Manhattan to meet this kid for when the time was right. We were all at Nancy's apartment one day and Ivan was answering my pager. He and Autumn were taking care of my business while I slept. The kid called and said he had the two cases I had been looking for so Ivan woke me up and told me it was on. I had heard this so many times so I didn't feel like going, but I got in the car. Autumn drove and I slept in the back. Now Ivan could do drugs all day and be fine, but he couldn't hold his liquor for shit.

When we all got to Midtown and they woke me up I saw Ivan had drank almost a whole 40 oz. of malt liquor, more than he could handle. I knew we were in trouble when Ivan put his gun on his waistband and it fell down his leg. Autumn stayed in the car and Ivan and I went into the apartment where the kids we were meeting were at. We get into the apartment and it is filled with club kids. The kid I had been dealing with told me his connect was on the way, so we waited. The ravers were partying and they offered me drugs, but I declined because I was there to pull a job. Ivan on the other hand decided he would join the fun. No matter how many dirty looks I gave him, he kept trying whatever they offered.

The time had come and the connect had arrived. The connect was a kid who called himself Scotty bottles. He looked like Slim Shady with facial piercings, but he wasn't a street dude and had no business selling drugs. This kid let us load all the drugs into our bags and talk these guys into the hallway. When we got into the hallway, Ivan made it for the stairs. The two guys followed Ivan and on the first landing going down the stairs, Ivan went for his gun and almost fell down. I had pulled out and had them so scared it looked like they were trying to hold the ceiling up. At that moment, the apartment door opened and a girl named Kitty Kat was standing at the door. When I looked her way, she slammed the door. She was smart. I let the two idiots walk past me back to the apartment and Ivan and I were on our way. Ivan and I set Scotty bottles up three more times before I ran him out of the business and took his connect. I saw Kitty Kat again when Matt was selling her drugs outside of a club, and she looked shocked and said, "You're that boy" as she realized who I was.

Scotty's connect was a guy from Staten Island named Rob. Rob would end up calling me and would try to set me up to get me killed. Rob called me up bitching about what I did and how he wanted his money. I told him I didn't owe him money because he needed to get the money from the dudes who couldn't hold their work. Rob tells me he's interested in buying some Crystal Meth from me. I knew he was trying to line me up, but I agreed to meet him anyway. Chris was at the house and I told him we were going to Staten Island. Autumn cried the whole ride. Chris had his favorite shotgun and I had a 9mm on me. Before I got to the Unicorn Diner where this meeting was taking place, I told Chris, "When I get out of the car, don't be seen and if I start shooting in their car, just hose the car down." This wasn't a very smart plan, but it was the plan.

The 500 Benz pulled up and I got into the backseat. There were three dudes in the car. Rob was driving, an old Italian was sitting shotgun and Johnny Poppo was in the backseat. Johnny later received 8 life sentences in the Feds for a bunch of mob murders. Johnny and I kept looking at each other until we both realized we knew one another. We realized we had been together in one of my youth prison stays and back then, we were friends. Due to this, their plans changed. They told me how they were going to kill me and I had Chris show them their plan may not have worked out. Mutual respect was eventually had by all. The last time Ivan and I would rob Scotty Bottles, it would be a set up by Rob where the drugs were given back to him, as a show of good faith on a new business venture.

Ivan, Richie and I got the address from Rob and armed with a crowbar and 3 guns, Scotty Bottles caught a rude awakening at 4am. With the door pried open, we rushed the apartment. I football tackled Scotty as he was trying to get out of his bed, and dragged him into the living room. We found a roll of duct tape and taped Scotty to the wall. We also found a polaroid camera and took pictures we thought were hysterical. Later the District Attorney didn't find the pictures so funny and would use them against me, but at the time, a dude taped to a wall with us posing around him with guns drawn seemed funny. Remember, I wasn't the smartest boy.

We got all the drugs, a nice stash of cash that I gave to Ivan and Richie, plus Ivan filled two duffle bags with stuff he wanted. I had only come to get the drugs so I could gain the connect. I now had a direct line on anything a drug dealer could need at the best prices in all of New York. Me and my team later would become the guns knows as BTS (Brooklyn Terror Squad). We were controlling the drug trade in every party we showed up at. I was putting party's together too, but I was always more interested in control of the drug trade within. The problem was, I was blatant with what I was doing and club owners would get nervous about doing business with me.

* * * * * *

Crystal was back involved in the business, but only the business. As much as she hated this, she had no choice because the money she and her father were making in NY, was too lucrative to pass up. If they wanted to operate in the NY club scene during this time, they had to go through me. Philly also needed drugs that had to come through me. The same guys I robbed when Crystal and I broke up, now needed to do business with me if they wanted to keep their supplies flowing. The Ecstasy market wasn't saturated like it is nowadays. You still had to know somebody to get large shipments of pills. Nowadays, a 16-year-old kid can get you 500 pills they are passing off as Ecstasy, but not in 1995. The quality of the pills was much better back then and we controlled the influx of Ecstasy so the prices stayed high. A single pill was $25-$30 and this made a nice chain of command for distribution because there was enough margin of profit for everyone involved to make money. I was the man who supplied the distributors. It took at least three people to run my part of the business. Matt, Autumn, Chris and I would be running to meet people all day and night. The problem with me was, I was usually too wasted to do much.

I was making money hand over fist, but I was also losing a lot of money too. I was a train wreck and my drug habit was out of control. I was always on so many drugs so I started carrying a little notebook where I listed everyone who owed me and everyone I gave things to. Yet, there would be times I would be so fucked up on drugs, I wouldn't keep track in the book. There were guys who would hand me money and I had no clue where it came from. I would pretend to remember these transactions but most of the time I was in a blacked-out state.

I loved money, but at this point in my life, it didn't have value. Yet, if someone shorted me, I would become violent to get what was owed to me. Looking back, it doesn't make any sense to me how I would blow money like it didn't matter, but then be ready to assault someone who had slighted me even the least. My drug habit caused me to lose hundreds of thousands of dollars just from being careless. If I counted the drugs I ingested, and considered free, and turned that into profit, it would have been in the millions.

* * * * * *

I hadn't seen any of my family members in well over a year. I didn't care if I lived or died, and at this point in my life, the way I was living made that clear. One of my family members got ahold of Autumn's phone number and called her to invite us to Easter dinner at Grandma's house. Autumn was very excited with the idea of meeting my family, so she accepted the invitation.

I went to the Florist and ordered two floral arrangements of Dutch Orchids and Tulips in beautiful vases. They were $200 each so I got one for my mother and one for my Grandmother. I had some weed for my Uncles and a pocket full of small bills to spread around to my cousins who were still little kids. I threw on a pair of Polo khakis, a nice Nautica sweater and a pair of glasses to conceal my bloodshot eyes. I decided to tone my jewelry down, but I kept the gold teeth in. Autumn got herself all done up. She was a hot little number, but she looked more like a stripper than a girl you bring home to meet the family. Right before we left, I got high so I wouldn't be drug sick for Easter dinner.

Once we got into the car, I had to explain a few things to Autumn. Autumn was a vegetarian and had been her entire life. I told Autumn how there wasn't going to be any fish at Grandma's. Grandma would be making ham and I would not allow her to disrespect my Grandmother's table. I said, "I don't care if you have to throw it up, but you're going to eat or at least make it look like you're eating." She said, "But I've never eaten meat in my life." I didn't care. Grandma was old school and I didn't want her to think I was with some weird girl. Autumn agreed to the terms, but I think she was starting to get the idea this was not going to be like the Easter Dinners she saw on TV.

We finally arrived at Grandma's and as Autumn parked the car, I took one more toot of dope. Autumn cleaned off my face with a baby wipe and made sure I didn't have any dope on my nose. We each grabbed one of the Floral arrangements and walked towards the house. We entered through the back door that lead to the kitchen and Grandma, my mom and my Aunt Annie were in there cooking. My cousins, brother and sisters were running around and it was so difficult to tell who was who at first because they were flying by so fast.

I locked eyes with Grandma and started to walk towards her to give her the flowers. Grandma caught me by surprise though. She placed the vase on the Kitchen table and slapped me once really good on the cheek, then offered her cheek for a kiss. I wasn't sure what I got hit for, it could have been many reasons. I introduced Autumn to everyone and gave my mom a kiss and her flowers. It was good to be home and other than the crack in the mouth, everyone seemed happy enough to see me.

After we said hello to everyone, I showed Autumn around the house and explained who were in the pictures. I showed Autumn off to my Uncles and then dropped her in the kitchen with the women and my mother's husband John. Autumn looked nervous, but it was sink or swim with the de Leyer women and after all, she was the one who wanted to come.

I went back into the library and my Uncles were in there watching TV. We bullshitted like guys do in a locker room. I was bragging about my sexual escapades and my Uncles were calling me a liar. I may have been playing it up a little bit for the crowd, but we were having fun. It was good to be with my family and have a little normal time, or as normal as my family time could get. My Uncles and I smoked some weed until it was time to eat.

When I walked over to the table, Autumn looked happy to see me. The de Leyer women can be a tough crowd. The table was loaded with thick slices of Honey Ham, Mashed Potatoes with fried onion, garlic and cheese, asparagus with Hollandaise sauce, sweet corn and Salad. Grandma led a quick prayer and it was time to dig in. I was proud of Autumn because she managed to pull off looking like she was eating everything. My family talked about the horse business and I chimed in when it was appropriate. Certain aspects of my life at that time were not appropriate for the Easter dinner table. Everyone knew by this point how I earned my living, but I was home and that is what was important. When I was with my family, I was not proud of what I did and how I lived my life. In the streets, my life was a badge of honor, but when I was home, I realized I was supposed to be so much more.

Dinner was finished and Grandma and the team were clearing the dirty dishes and preparing for coffee and dessert. Through the library there were glass doors that led out to the back patio. My Uncles and I went outside and lit up a joint when suddenly, the doors busted open and it was my baby sister Cassie. We were chasing her off when she said, "My daddy said you're bad and you're a drug dealer." My Uncles and I didn't find this funny at all. My Uncles looked at me and said, "John told her that shit and she is probably running around school saying this. Who does he think he is? This is Grandma's house, your house!" I was pissed off that this idiot would tell my baby sister this crap. At the time, she was only around seven years old. My Uncles knew what they were doing, they wanted to see a fight and they didn't like John. My mother was the only one who liked him.

I stormed into the dining room where John was sitting with the women, and sat down next to Autumn. Autumn could sense something was wrong so she tried to grab my hand under the table, but I pushed her away and locked eyes on John. My other family members were still speaking about business, but my Uncles were standing in the doorway watching. Without me even having to instigate John said, "Maybe we could all take a tip from Jeff on the positive aspects of free enterprise." John was the only one who thought his comments were funny and this was the "in" I needed. I jumped up and said, "I've had enough of your shit you bitch. This is my family's house and you come in here disrespecting me? Cassie just came into the library saying I'm bad and I am a drug dealer. What the fuck gives you the right to put this shit in her head? Take your ass outside, I am going to beat your ass." I was ready to go.

Grandma doesn't play and she is not going to allow anyone to get out of line in her house, Grandma will be respected. Grandma walked over and told John, "It is time to go outside now. Men's work is men's work at the end of the day." If we were fighting in the house, Grandma was getting involved and Grandma was Gangster. My mom was crying and my Uncles were egging on the fight. My Uncles loved live action and fights at the de Leyer house were not unusual. I already had fights with John at this point in my life. I may have had a crazy drug habit, but I had also been to jail, prison, shootouts, and brawls. This was stock and trade in the streets. My whole life was about engaging in physical combat and back then, I was young and loved the action.

John was around 6'2", played baseball, rode horses and he had some weight on him, but he was 40 something and was not a fighter. I didn't care if it was Easter. This man disrespected me at my family's house and I hated him. I hated him for being with my mom and changing her. The fight didn't last very long. He may have gotten off a couple of shots, but before long he was on his back with me on top of him. I stopped when Grandma said it was over.

The wedge between my mother and I grew wider, but I was so messed up on drugs, I didn't see it back then. I was able to see my family and this was all that mattered to me. This was the last time I ever saw my mother in the streets, the next time I saw her I was in prison.

* * * * * *

My main function in my business was to show up when it was time to talk to the major players. Autumn was well organized and smart enough to make everything run. My reputation and name kept the business running, but I was more concerned with chasing bitches and getting high. I had a $500 a day drug habit. I would sniff 3 or 4 bags of dope just to get out of bed and then I would ride one of my dirt bikes for an hour or so on the track, not far from our house. 3 or 4 bags of Heroin would cause most people to end up in a comma, but all it did to me was prevent me from getting sick and keep me as normal as I could be. The problem with opiate addiction is, sooner or later it takes more and more to get you high and if you don't have the drug, you get violently ill.

My business was thriving as was my love life. I was living with Autumn, I had Heidi and another girl named Larice. Larice's brother worked for me. I had met Larice at the Roxy in Manhattan when I saw her dancing and she was a blonde haired blue-eyed beauty. Larice's mother had cancer and was at the end of her life and Larice and her brother were doing what they could to keep their household afloat. I respected this and helped them where I could. Larice's mother's cancer was at the stage where she was crazy and she would scream and curse at me. I was a big bad gangster and had survived numerous shootouts, however, I feared her mother. Larice had a job, was going to college and studied as a dancer. I would fall asleep at the house and Larice would leave to go wherever her day was taking her. When I would finally wake up, I was afraid to leave the room, fearing confrontation with the mother.

Autumn put up with my cheating as long as I knew where home was. Autumn and I were living in Long Island in a nice neighborhood in the suburbs. Our house had a pool in the backyard on the deck. Our neighbors hated us because there was traffic all hours of the day and night, plus, I would race up and down the street on my toys. I started getting the feeling I was being followed and I was right. I knew the police were on me, but I couldn't stop doing what I was doing. My guys relied on me to keep them supplied and my connects needed me to keep the work moving. I was a key player in the game and the fact that I had an expensive lifestyle, also forced me to keep going.

One night I was out partying and on my way home, I stopped at a diner in Smithtown to grab a takeout order. I was in the middle of placing my order when I looked over to a group of girls sitting at a booth, and I couldn't believe who I saw. It was Joy. I hadn't seen her in almost 2 years. I will never forget the look she gave me when she realized it was me. It was a completely emotionless blank stare, like she saw ghost or something. I cracked a half smile, grabbed my food and got the hell out of there. My car was loaded with club whores and I was no longer the boy she once knew. I was so far gone and so fucked up on drugs, it fucked me up to see her. I didn't even speak to her.

I would never see her as a free man again. This was over 20 years ago, but I remember this night as it was yesterday. Looking back now, I didn't speak to Joy because I was ashamed of who I had become. I didn't want her to see this was me, I didn't want her to see how the drugs and my lifestyle, had fully taken over. She was someone who knew a different me, and at this point in my life, the boy she knew was gone.

* * * * * *

On June 26, 1996, Crystal and Autumn's mother were visiting at the house, while I was sleeping in the den in the basement. Autumn got into the car and was going to the store to get food for when I woke up when she was pulled over a block from our house. The cops told her they were about to raid the house, and they wanted to know who was inside and where the pit bulls and guns were. Things were about to get really bad for me and I was fast asleep.

"Nobody move, police!" There isn't anything in the world that fucks your sleep up like a tactical drug swat team, kicking down your door. I jumped up off the sectional couch half asleep, hoping I was dreaming. As I looked up the stairwell, I stood in disbelief as I watched at least 20 Swat Officers rushing through the house. Autumn's poor mother Lynn was on her way to the pool when the swat team breached the door. She was so afraid, she peed in her bathing suit. Crystal was sunbathing on the deck when I was immediately tackled onto the couch and handcuffed.

Forget the fact that my house was being raided and I was in an asshole of trouble, all I was thinking about was how I wouldn't be able to get high. I wasn't quite sure what they were after, because my life was filled with so many felony activities and by this point, I didn't care. I just sat and listened to the officers smashing holes in my walls and watched them rip the den apart. One officer came downstairs laughing and said, "Hey guys, my wife gave me $5 for lunch, yet this asshole has over $40,000 just sitting in the sock drawer." By the time I was led up the stairs, my kitchen table was filled with drugs, money, ringing cell phones and beepers. The phones in the house were ringing off the hook, and it started to sink in how I was in a lot of trouble. I was later escorted upstairs where I had to argue with the officers just for them to allow me to get a pair of sneakers.

The officers had already taken Autumn and Crystal and thankfully, they didn't arrest Autumn's mother. I was eventually escorted out of the house and down the driveway to the cop car. All the nosy housewives were standing on their front lawns watching as I was placed into the police car. I heard the applause of crowd as they stood cheering and clapping as we pulled off. I was on my way to jail.

ELEVEN

SICK TO DEATH

"History doesn't repeat itself, but it does rhyme"
-Mark Twain

I had a good run, but it was now over. I was brought to the Nassau Narcotics Unit and I had warrants all over for cases I had never shown up to court for. Lynn had called my Lawyer the minute the police left and he showed up at the precinct shortly after. I had been smart enough to keep an attorney on retainer. My life was being destroyed and I felt like death.

After hours of interrogation, and one day in the processing pens, not only was my life coming to an end, my drug habit was rearing its ugly head. My stomach was turning, I was experiencing severe hot and cold flashes and my bones hurt. I couldn't stop throwing up and I had constant diarrhea. I was shaking so badly, because my body was craving the drugs I had spent years ingesting. This is called being "dope sick".

For four days, I wished I would die because death at that point, would've been better than what I was going through. I was unable to get high that morning because I was asleep and now I wasn't going to get any drugs. I spent my first few days in jail, kicking my Heroin addiction.

I was in the papers and the talk of the county jail because not many guys get arrested with two girls who could have easily posed in playboy. Crystal and Autumn had both gotten out on bail but I was denied bail, because my history of jumping bail made me ineligible. The cops finally had me with severe enough charges that I was going to prison. They knew if they set bail, I would have made it and took off. I was really trying to get the lawyer to get me a bail so I could run. If I would have made bail, I would have run.

After they started the main case in Nassau County, they started shipping me to Queens and Suffolk County to answer old warrants. In Suffolk County I had the old warrants, plus the new case for everything that was found in the house. My lawyer loved me because all my problems cost me enough to buy him a summer house and I paid my legal costs in cold hard cash. Autumn's lawyer didn't want her visiting me, yet she was there all three visits every week. I had gotten a job where I swept, mopped and took care of the cell block. This is known in prison as being the Porter. Having a job in prison allowed me to get a fourth visit. I used this visit for the girlfriends, Heidi one week, Larice next week. What a piece of shit I was. Autumn had caught a serious case because of me and I was still fucking around with other girls.

My 20th Birthday came and Autumn had to see her Lawyer so Lynn showed up with a homemade T-shirt that said, "Happy Birthday". The shirt had a cake and candles on it. It was cute and made me feel loved. Jail was good to me. I started working out really hard and I was blowing up. I had worked out when I was young playing sports and when I was in juvenile prison. I was also going to school so I could obtain my GED. The problem was, I was also receiving another kind of education. Prison didn't scare me enough to go straight. Instead, I was planning my future crimes the entire time I was locked up.

Matt and the rest of my guys were all still in the streets, and it was business as usual. I was on the phone with my guys every day and everyone was just waiting for me to come home. I was going through problems with the courts though. My first offer was 8 ½ - 25. I wasn't going for that. The lawyer got them to offer 4 to Life and then 3 to Life. I had class A felonies and this was a standard offer under New York States Rockefeller Drug Laws, but I still wasn't trying to hear anything with life on the end of the sentence. Looking back on the choices I made when I got out, I should have taken the 8 ½ -25 because I may have learned my lesson, but this is not how it happened.

I called the DA's bluff and told my lawyer I wanted to go to trial. I didn't know much about the law, but I knew I paid my lawyers a lot of money and I planned on making them work for it. My first break came in the Suffolk case. Something was wrong with the search warrant and the judge's signature. I don't really know because the District Attorney who was helping with the case had the most perfect ass, and I paid more attention to her, then what was going on. The hormones of a 20-year-old boy. All I knew was, things started going in my favor.

The problem with their case was, the cops making the case against me were from Nassau County, and every time the guy who got pinched and made a deal to wear a wire on me, talked to me while I was in Suffolk County. All the sales took place in Nassau County. Autumn had delivered the drugs for me a bunch of times while Matt or Chris was with her. The cop's problem was, neither Matt or Chris were in custody nor did they know who they were. Nassau claimed they had me on camera selling 25 mls of LSD. I had no clue if I was there and I knew I very well could have been. The DA was banking on the fact that he had me on a direct sale, because he had video and audio of the sale in question. The problem for them was, when my lawyer and I got to review the video, it wasn't me. It was Matt. They were fucked. I wasn't going to give my best friend up and their case against me was falling apart. My problem was, they had Autumn dead to right.

I could have beat the case, but Autumn would be stuck holding everything and I am not that much of a piece of shit. The DA pulled me to court without my lawyers and had me brought to his office in the presence of the lead narcotics detective. They laid it down for me and I was told I could beat the case, but if I did, my girlfriend was going to prison. They also told me they had been listening to my calls in the county jail and they knew I was still involved and if I beat the case, they would do everything in their power to take me down. I was then told they would drop the A felonies down to B's if I would take a cop-out. If I took the cop-out in both counties, they would run everything together and Autumn could get life probation and not have to go to jail or prison. I didn't care about the felony convictions and I wasn't about to let Autumn go down for my business.

* * * * * *

Karla had recently moved back to New York and she heard I was locked up. She eventually decided to bring my daughter to see me. I still wasn't 100% sure she was mine, but I wanted to see the baby. Our first visit was the first time I ever saw Alexis. Karla started bringing the baby up once a week and I enjoyed spending time with her. When I would go back to my cell, I would really think about what I should do. I felt like Alexis deserved to have a mother and father who were together, but I also felt like I owed Autumn because I was such a dick when I was with her. I was torn between who I owed more to; the one who helped me run my empire, or the one I had a baby with.

Autumn would bring Karla money from my stash so she could get Alexis things she needed, but this became an issue for Karla. She felt the nice things Autumn had should have been hers because she was the mother of my child. However, she wasn't my girl and she had her own man. I had said things to Karla on the visit I shouldn't have and I wrote her a letter stating we should be together due to the baby. Karla immediately contacted Autumn the moment she received the letter. Karla has always wanted what Karla wanted. She didn't want to be with me, she had a live-in boyfriend. Karla just didn't want any other woman to be with me. Me being me, I fast talked my way out of everything with Autumn until she finally got tired of my shit and we broke up.

Autumn and Heidi had a fight in front of the jail due to Karla starting nonsense. After this, Karla's boyfriend had an issue with me calling the house and speaking to her about the baby. Karla had issues and I didn't have time for them, so I spent the rest of my time in prison without seeing or speaking to my daughter.

* * * * * *

I was eventually shipped to Suffolk County Jail and was locked down due to the amount of fighting and bullshit I did on my last two trips. I got to see the beautiful DA one last time, she looked quite splendid in her pantsuit and I was sentenced. I was taken back to Nassau because I had already closed my Queens cases. Nassau County was where this started and it would be the last place on the journey before I would be shipped upstate to prison. One morning, about a month after I had been sentenced, I was told to pack up because my bus was waiting.

30 or 40 of us were loaded onto a prison style Greyhound bus and carted off to a down-state correctional facility. All the new arrivals get their heads shaved, strip searched, forfeit all their belongings and are then issued their new state items. Three pairs of green pants, three green button-up short sleeve shirts, three pairs of underclothes, one white button-up church shirt, a pair of fake converse and a pair of cheap work boots.

In prison, almost everyone is affiliated in some way or another whether it be a gang or a religious group. In one of my college papers, I wrote about religious gangs in prison. In New York State, prisons have Bloods, Crips, Latin Kings, Netas and many other gangs. I didn't come to prison looking to become a gang member, but I ended up being recruited because of my loyalty to some of my guys who happened to be bangin.

In Downstate reception prison, I had run into a kid I had grown up with. Wendell had come upstate on a robbery charge from Rikers Island. Wendell and I had ended up getting on the same bus once we left downstate, headed to Green Correctional Facility. On the bus, Wendell met up with another Blood member who was also going to the same prison. In the early to mid-90's, the Blood movement within New York was just starting to grow. The Netas and Latin Kings organizations were the strongest movements.

Green prison was controlled by these two gangs and Bloods were not welcome in this prison. Wendell's homie had already been upstate serving his bid, unlike Wendell and I who were fresh upstate. On the bus, Wendell was told they were going to have issues in Green. When we arrived, those of us who were going to Green got off the bus and we were lead to the prisons clinic unit to be cleared. While we were waiting, we were brought lunch by a Spanish inmate and he used a Blood Salutation he said, "031". Wendell and the other homie replied, "All the time". (031 is a Blood salutation from one homie to another letting them know that you respect them as being Blood. All the time is the acknowledgement.) The Spanish kid laughed and stated, "We got you papa" and he left. That little interaction let the two gang members know they were going to have problems.

All the new recruits were brought to the reception cottages. The compound was made up of cottages and those cottages housed the inmates. Wendell and I didn't have much property, just what we were issued from reception. However, the homie had personal property he had amassed in the time he was upstate. All his personal clothing was red, being the color of his gang affiliation. Wendell was my friend and this kid was his homie, so I felt like he was now my friend and I always held my friends down. In prison, you watch your friends backs and you expect the same.

I wasn't gang related yet, but I was loyal and I've never been a coward. At this point in my life, I was 20 years old and 205 lbs. of solid muscle. I have always been able to fight, but I was also stronger than I had ever been before. The homie gave us each a hoodie because it was still cold, and we didn't have clothes for the weather. The hoodies were red of course and when you wear red in prison, you are assumed Blood.

The homie had a gem star razor that he broke in half so Wendell and him both had weapons. I didn't have anything, but I didn't need a weapon, I had my hands.

You could feel the tension and we sensed plotting. I wasn't Blood yet, but I was as far as the inmates were concerned because of the fact we were together. We all went outside to the recreation yard and we took a walk around together to see the layout and then went over to the pull up bar, so we could get a couple of sets in. The plan was, one of us does our set, while the other two keep an eye out for the attack. I was on the pull up bar doing my set when our assailants started to make their move. The guys looked at me and said, "Here it comes" and I was ready, but when I jumped off the pull-up bar and turned around I got nervous. There was a group of 10-12 guys coming our way. We didn't wait, we were outnumbered and the best defense is a strong offense so we ran into the crowd and fought as best we could. In the heat of battle, it is hard to know what is happening because everything happens so fast.

We fought until the officers eventually broke everything up. I had some cuts and bruises but I was alright. We were handcuffed and escorted to the special housing unit where we would be locked up. In prison, when an inmate gets into trouble, they are brought before an administration official who will decide what your punishment will be. We were all sent to Coxsackie Correctional Facility to serve out our punishments. Coxsackie is a Maximum-Security Prison that houses a lot of New York States younger inmates. This would be my first trip to Coxsackie, but not my last.

Once we got out of lock-up I was introduced to the Bloods that were in prison. Coxsackie was wild during this time. It seemed like every time we came out of our cells, something was going down. I was a young man and the action excited me. I was in the facility for a few months, until I was transferred back to another medium security prison. I was sent to a prison called Ogdensburg. Ogdensburg prison is located on the border of Canada. The bridge from the United States into

Canada can be seen from the recreation yard. As soon as I got to the prison, I saw a guy I had an issue with from Nassau County Jail. He worked in the prison mess hall and was a member of the gang "the Netas". In prison, telling another man to suck your dick are fighting words. I told this guy in front of everyone on the chow line to "suck my dick". I wanted to fight this guy because I felt like our problems were unresolved and now that he had added a couple of pounds of muscle, he was trying to act tough. By me telling him to suck my dick, I was forcing his hand.

In the prison, there were men who I knew. The black kids I grew up with, their Uncle Malik was in the prison and he introduced me as family even though I was white. I told Malik about my issue with this guy. He told me he would make sure I didn't get jumped. I came out to the gym and Malik talked to the guy who was the head of the Netas for the prison. The set up was, I would go into the bathroom and me and this guy would fight. Malik told the guys if anything funny happened in the bathroom there would be problems. Malik gave me a pair of cowhide skin mittens and told me to make him proud.

I went into the bathroom area with this kid and about four of his gang buddies. The bathroom was large and the officers couldn't see inside. I got patted down to make sure I didn't have a weapon concealed. Standing like two boxers in the middle of a ring, we squared off. Sucking his teeth, he said, "I've been waiting for this moment since the county. That shit you did in the county ain't gonna happen again." I thought this was funny because I had already beat the crap out of him twice in the county. I looked at him, laughed in his face and said, "I'm gonna beat your pussy ass like I did the other times."

The fight didn't go much different than the first two. The kid swung wild, I slipped out of the way and hit him with two clean shots and he was out on his feet. I didn't let him get off that easy though because I pushed him against the wall and used my shoulder to hold him up and caught a few more shots off as he slid down the wall. When he hit the ground, I started to stomp him when one of his buddies grabbed me. I turned on him and hit him with two shots that put him to sleep as well. I looked at the others and said, "Ya'll want some too?" The guys backed up and gave me room to leave. I strutted out of the bathroom feeling myself.

I went to the bleachers where Malik and his people were waiting for me and Malik said, "What happened kid?" I said, "Two of them are laid out in the bathroom." Malik said, "Did they try to jump you?" I said, "I don't know, but after I beat the first one's ass, his man tried to grab me and I leveled him as well." A couple of minutes later the Netas came over to the bleachers to make sure everything was over and said, "You have to respect him because at least he came in and fought you like a man." I said, "I ain't gotta respect shit and he can suck my dick." Malik said, "Be easy kid, let me deal with this." I shut my mouth and let Malik deal with the prison politics that surrounded this situation. In prison, everything gave cause for men to want to politic.

I spent the rest of my time in that prison working out, eating, going on visits, and preparing for my return to the streets. I earned my GED and I was later granted parole. I left all my property to Malik and was shipped out to Queensboro prison in the city. In Queensboro, I worked out, watched TV, cut hair in the barbershop, talked to everyone on the phone and did my best to make time pass. I had what they called an "or earlier date". This gave me a release date, but as soon as my information cleared I could be released whenever.

I was cutting hair in the barbershop when I came out and saw everyone looking at a list on the wall. My name was the second one on the list. I looked over to the group of guys and said, "What's this list for?" One of the guys said, "If your name is on the list you go home tomorrow." I had been waiting 18 months for this day to come. It was hard to believe it was happening.

Autumn and I had broken up and I was dealing with a girl named Kristen. She was Matt's ex and used to be Autumn's friend until she found out we were fucking before I got arrested. Kristen had shown up every week to see me. Kristen was finishing college to become a fashion designer and when she would show up on the visit, she would shut it down. This girl came downstate to see me in an evening gown and another time in a mink coat and leather pants. Kristen had bought me the outfit I was to wear the day of my release, but the clothes were sent to Ogdensboro before I left. The clothes were supposedly shipped down to Queensboro, but they hadn't arrived yet. With my "or earlier date", I didn't have clothes. After I saw my name of the list, I called Kristen and said, "You need to go buy me another pair of Wallabees, linen pants and shirt." Kristen said, "I called the prison and they said the clothes will be transferred to you." I cut her off and said, "I'm coming home tomorrow so you need to take off work and come get me."

I couldn't sleep that night. In the morning, they hadn't processed my clothes so I was given a sweatshirt and still jeans and I was pissed off. While everyone was getting dressed, I sat in the waiting room area with my friend from the Bronx drawing. I had been talking my big money shit and now I was leaving prison dressed as they send the homeless out the door.

I was the second one to get called to leave. When I was called, I got my check with the money that was in my inmate account and I walked out the door into a light rain. Kristen hit the horn on her brand-new Infiniti G20. Kristen and one of my top guys Jeff, who would later betray me, jumped out of the car. I kissed Kristen, Jeff put my chain around my neck, handed me a stack of cash and gave me a hug. I stripped out of the prison clothes as guys were coming out the door. Once dressed I got behind the wheel and replayed Jay Z's "The City Is Mine" again and again. I wanted everyone in that room to see me. I was a young man and cared what guys I would never see again thought of me.

The building Mariel lived in was around the corner from where I was released. We all went to the diner that was on the end of Mariel's block. I knew everyone who worked in that diner and my waitress happened to be Mariel's friend. I wanted her to tell Mariel I was home and how I looked. Like I said, I was very vain. Kristen then brought me out to Grandma's house on Long Island. Grandma had always been my number one supporter and I had to see her right away. At Grandma's, I made calls to the boys and plans for them to come by and talk business. Kristen was not happy about this because she really wanted me to go straight. I should have, but I was young and still very much in love with the streets. I hadn't done enough time in prison to get it all out of my system.

* * * * * *

My family never showed up at court and they didn't visit me while I was in prison, but I would call my mother weekly to check in. She would speak to me and lecture me about getting my life together when I got home. Being classic Jeff, I listened to my mother and told her what she wanted to hear. My mother's friend Sheila lined me up with a job in Manhattan at a commercial advertising agency. Not bad, considering I only had a prison GED and was on parole.

The producer was a friend of the family and I used to ride her horse when I was a kid so she gave me a shot as a production assistant. There was no interview, my interview was she knew my family. They even wrote letters of recommendation on my behalf when I went before the parole board. I lived part time in Manhattan with friends of my family. JFK Jr and Woody Allen lived on our block. I still had an apartment in Jackson Heights, Queens and I would spend a night or two at Grandma's. Everyone was glad I was home and I was off the drugs. I got two memberships to gyms so I could continue to work out. I even had the boys get involved.

The night I came home my inner circle came to see me. I was given three kilos to get back on my feet in the game. I still had some money that I had to pick up from Autumn, and at Grandma's there was also a stash, but lawyers and prison had put a nice dent in my nest egg. I still had Sammy and Gill, my connects who had worked with Dom, Mark and Matt while I was gone. But I wanted the rave scene back, and I was ready to strong arm my way back in if need be. While in prison, the BTS crew (Brooklyn Terror Squad) had about 350 of these kids from all over and the boys were recruiting at the raves. I knew about this because they were writing me about it while I was in prison. I would use this gang to seize power once again. The Boss was home and my mind was focused. Frank Owens the writer would later do an article in Details magazine titled "The Ecstasy Bandits". I wouldn't talk because I had never told the story until now. Plus, at the time, I was on Rikers Island fighting my murder case.

I had come home and it was as if I hadn't left, and the fact that most of these people didn't do anything to help me while I was in prison, didn't even cross my mind. I was sleeping with strippers and club girls every single night because I was trying to make up for the time I was gone. The old me was back just minus the drug habit. The money was coming in but I was back on my cowboy shit. When I came home, there were new players in the game. I had come home on a Thursday and the next night I was at Club Carbon. The week after, I tricked the new Israeli Ecstasy connect into the car, held him at gunpoint with the boys, while I talked to his brother and made them take me on as a partner. I was up to my old tricks once again.

After tending to business late one night I had Kristen drive me out to Grandma's house. I was getting ready to put money in one of my hiding places so I was counting the stacks and placing them on the kitchen table. I had taken my gun off because I was at Grandma's. During this time, My Uncle Marty was staying at Grandma's house because his wife had kicked him out. It was the middle of the night and I was sitting at the kitchen table next to the wall. Kristen was sitting at another chair on the side of the table, when in walks a very drunk Uncle Marty. Men who work on horse farms all their lives are tough old men who have strong heavy hands. Uncle Marty was the miserable drunk version of the Marlboro Man, and he was without a question, a tough old man.

162

Uncle Marty was apparently feeling rowdy. The first words out of his mouth were, "All of those muscles and you're still a little bitch" Now remember, I am fresh home from prison. I am 205lbs of solid twenty-one-year-old muscle. The only reason I was tough was because around my uncles, you had to be tough. I said, "Why don't you take your drunk ass to sleep." My uncle came back with, "you ain't tell this pretty girl how big bubba was fucking you in your ass in prison." Now my uncles are no strangers to jail. They know these are fighting words to a twenty-one-year-old me.

Before I could get out of my chair, I was socked in the mouth with a punch that felt like a mule had kicked me. The truth of the matter was, if not for the wall next to my seat I would've been on my ass. I was a good fighter, but I knew I didn't want another one of those shots so I grabbed the gun from the table and backed my uncle up. Uncle Marty wasn't scared because he knew I wouldn't shoot him but he didn't hit me again. My uncle said, "What are you going to do? Shoot me you little bastard?" I said, "Stop fucking around or I will shoot you in your leg and you won't be going to work in the morning."

Now Grandma had eight children, six of them boys, and they didn't fuck with the boss. I didn't hear Grandma come through the pantry behind me, but I sure felt her when she cracked me with that riding crop. Grandma was on me like Zorro raining down really accurate shots. I dropped the gun and got out of her way. One of the many great things about Grandma was, she was fair. It didn't matter how this started, we were both getting it. Once she was finished with me, she was on to my uncle. She cracked him enough to regain control of the situation.

Not even out of breath, Grandma laid down the law and said, "Marty get down stairs and go to sleep and Jeff, it is time for the girl to go home." Grandma's terms were never negotiable. Kristen was scared to death and shaking. When I walked her to her car she was trying to make sense out of what she had witnessed. To me this was all normal, but to her this was out of her league. I sent her home and went back inside. When I came back into the kitchen Grandma was heating up the plate she had for me in the fridge. She said, "Eat, you look hungry then lock up and go to sleep." I did as I was told.

The next day I had to report to my parole officer. In the morning when I looked in the mirror I had all sorts of whip marks on my face which made me look like the victim of an S&M situation gone wrong. Grandma had to bring me to parole since she sent Kristen home. When I was with my parole officer he said, "What happened to your face?" I said, "My Grandmother hit me with a horse whip." He looked at me for a minute, puzzled and confused and I could tell he was wrestling with the question of why, but I guess he decided he didn't want to know. He said, "Was there any police contact?" I said, "No" He said, "Can you piss in a cup?" I said, "Yes." I got back into the car with Grandma and we were on our merry way.

* * * * * *

While I was in prison I had recruited a crew of new misfits to get involved. I was getting everyone involved because I needed to be able to set guys up, to rob my competition. I'd let the guys keep the drugs and money because I was having these robberies done to hurt the drug dealers who sold drugs in the areas where I had business interests. I had all sorts of guys who just wanted to be a part of our thing because everyone was making money. I knew how to keep my guys happy and loyal. I was working diligently to build a criminal empire. I bought myself a new Infiniti Q-45 the third week home.

I had been home a few weeks before I went to see Autumn to get my money. I pulled into the parking of her dorm and waited until she came downstairs. As soon as I saw her, I said, "Where the fuck is my money bitch?" She said, "So you're not coming upstairs?" With sex on my mind, I had forgotten about the money and agreed to go upstairs. I had told my boys if they called and I didn't answer they knew what was up. Autumn's father had bought out her dorm room, so she didn't have a roommate. As soon as we walked in, I was all over her.

Autumn was playing around buying time. When the phone rang, I said, "Don't answer it" But she said, "I have to." She answered the phone and handed it to me. When I got on the phone, I said, "Give me a couple of minutes." Autumn told me, "If we are going to fuck, it isn't going to be a couple of minutes." At this point realizing I wasn't about to get any pussy, I got back down to business. I said, "Give me my money." I noticed the stupid look on her face. She retrieved a manila envelope that was clearly lighter than it should have been. I didn't need to count the money to know it wasn't all there. I snatched my money and left. Autumn knew what I was up to as soon as she saw my new car. Everyone knew what I was up to, because it was the same thing I was always up to. This would be the last time I ever saw Autumn.

* * * * * *

When I was released, I called Karla to schedule a day for her to bring the baby to Grandma's house. Grandma had never met the baby and I felt like the boss needed to meet her. During this time, my street life was so crazy, I didn't want anyone to know I had a daughter. I was never the type of criminal who would go after someone's family to get even with them, but I was now playing at a level where my enemies may have just done that.

The night Karla brought the baby, she had me sitting at Grandma's for over an hour waiting for her. Karla finally pulled up with her sister Randy and the baby. I went outside and was pissed off because Grandma was sleeping and now I had to wake her up, but I was excited to see Alexis where we could play and hangout. I was trying to not allow Karla to get under my skin, because I was so excited to see Alexis.

When she pulled the baby out of the car seat, she had a cigarette hanging out of her mouth and I flipped. I couldn't believe she was smoking with the baby in her arms. I knocked the cigarette out of her mouth and snatched the baby from her and we walked into the house. I will never forget asking the baby if she wanted juice and how cute she looked when she nodded her head yes as her blonde hair bounced everywhere. I left Karla and Randy in the kitchen and Alexis and I were off to play.

At Grandmas house on the side of the library there is a glass enclosed patio filled with toys for when her grandchildren came over. I went into the playroom with the baby and once the baby was situated, I ran upstairs and woke Grandma up. Grandma watched the baby play for a few minutes and said, "Come to Oma" in her thick Dutch accent. The funny thing was, the baby got up and went to her right away. Grandma scooped her up in her arms, gave her a kiss on each cheek and looked the baby over and said, "This is yours" and this was all I needed to hear.

The baby and I played with blocks and we made a little log cabin. We were just in our own little world. I loved to just watch her and hear her little giggle. Her giggle warmed my soul. I pulled the baby's shoes off and put her on the couch so we could watch "the fox and the hound" I asked Alexis if she wanted more juice and this time I received a squeaky "yes" and a big smile.

I walked back into the Kitchen and Randy was bent over with her head in the fridge and I was admiring her ass. Randy turned around and caught me looking and said, "What are you looking at?" I said, "I am looking at you and you look good as hell. What's up with that pussy?" Randy laughed as she put her hands on her hips and said, "You think you're so slick. You have a baby with my sister and I already know you're a piece of shit." I didn't let her slick comment faze me. I knew it was wrong, but I didn't care. Randy snatched the soda out of the fridge and walked past me with a "fuck you" look on her face. I laughed at her and said, "You know you want me." As I swatted her on her ass. I really thought I was a playboy.

I grabbed a juice box and a Heineken for myself and went back to the baby. I popped the straw in the juice box, pulled the coffee table close to the couch and put the baby on my chest. I had my beer and she had her juice and we were just cooling out. Halfway through the movie I looked down and the baby was asleep. I just looked at this little angel sleeping on my chest, and in that moment, there wasn't any other place I would rather be. I wanted to be a good father, I just didn't know how to be.

The Night That Changed My Life

It was a hot day in July and I had some business to attend to in Queens. I had handled so many drug deals in my lifetime, that this had become business as usual for me. But for some reason on this day, I had an unusual feeling in my gut that I just couldn't shake. I cocked the .380 I was carrying so if this deal got out of control, I would be ready.

This is something I had done hundreds of times, but this time the outcome would be different. I wish I would have paid attention to my gut feeling. If I had, two lives may have been saved that day. I may have been ready for what was about to happen, but I sure as hell wasn't ready for the repercussions of what would happen.

When I pulled up in that parking lot, I didn't realize I was crossing a line. Once again, I was traveling down the wrong path as I had so many times in my life, but this time, there would be no going back.

"Mr. de Leyer, do you have anything to say before I impose sentence?" "No sir." "Well Mr. de Leyer, I will keep the promise that I made. I'm not going to subject you to any lectures. I just want you to understand that this Court, of course, condemns what you did in the strongest of terms. There is some attempt here in some of the material that I've read to cast you in a sympathetic light. I do not see you in a sympathetic light, Mr. de Leyer. Very simply, you're a killer and you're getting a killer's sentence. The mitigation that you are receiving is, of course, mitigation from a potential death penalty that you faced and, of course, some mitigation from the maximum sentence you could have received under conviction for this crime.

169

Accordingly, Mr. de Leyer, it is the sentence of the Court that you be sentenced to the custody of the New York State Department of Correctional Services for an indeterminate term, the maximum of which shall be life, the minimum of which shall be 23 years. The mandatory surcharge is imposed. The money will come from inmate funds. Thank you very much counselors."

TWELVE

JOY & HEARTACHE

"I won't glorify or romanticize heartbreak. For me it was a kind of death, and I was forced to keep living" -Warsan Shire

The music was loud on the cellblock, the racket was so normal, that any seasoned inmate had the ability to tune out the noise. At this point in my life, I was 26 years old and I had already been in prison for 5 years, so I had no issue reading my book during the regular chaos. My cell was #17 out of 40 cells on the prison tier. I was in the middle but even through all the loud music and noise, I heard a woman's voice, "female walking on the company".

In prison, when a woman is on the cell block, they will announce their presence, so the men know to be dressed appropriately. Miss Scott was my inmate counselor and once every three months she called me into her office to check on my progress with my programs and such. When Miss Scott stopped in front of my cell it was a little bit of a shock.

However, the message she was about to deliver, was one I never saw coming.

After a quick greeting, Miss Scott told me a friend from my past, Joy had called and wanted to come visit me. I was excited and told Miss Scott to please tell her to come. Miss Scott gave me such a scare because she said she wasn't sure if she had kept her number, but God was on my side and Joy would make it up to see me. When she left from in front of my cell I laid back in my bed, my book forgotten and drifted back in time.

When Joy and I would hang out, I was always able to drop my tough guy persona. Joy would come with me and the boys when we would go surfing and she would sit on the beach and watch us surf for hours, even as late as November when we needed dry suits because it was so cold. She would come to the different Raves with me and we would run around Grandma's house like a couple of teenage kids. It was nice to be able to be normal, and she was the only one I could be normal with.

The last time I saw Joy, I was high as a kite at a diner in Smithtown. I was so messed up on drugs I didn't even speak to her, and now I would see her as an inmate housed in a Maximum-Security Prison in Upstate New York. My blonde surfer cut was replaced with long brown hair I mostly kept in braids. I wore my hair in braids because I was a gang member banging and without them, I would give my enemies an easy head of hair to hold onto. The cornrows kept my hair close to my scalp, plus I could hide razors in my braids. Prison is a dangerous place and gang members had to be ready to battle, whenever, wherever.

I was no longer the young boy she once knew, I had seen and been involved in too much. I was nervous to see this woman and I couldn't figure out what she could possibly want with me. After all, I was locked into a choice I had made a long time ago. Jeff de Leyer was no longer alive, I was now known as Dutch.

I made it through the night and even managed to sleep some. Early in the morning I was informed I had a visit. I shaved, took a shower and I went down to the visit room. As soon as I walked through the door I saw her and my god, she looked beautiful. She was cute as a

172

young woman, but as a grown woman she was absolutely breathtaking. I saw her, but she looked right through me because she was waiting for someone and I wasn't him. I walked over to the officer's station and checked in. I wasn't as handsome as I was as a kid, so I had to make up for it with my charm. I put a little extra bop in my step and I made my way over to the table.

When I was standing over her I said, "Are you looking for someone?" She looked at me puzzled and after she erased the years of hard living off my face she found who she had come to see. She was speechless and covered her mouth in shock and said, "Oh my god Jeff!" I sat down, and we started to talk. It was obvious to me she was uncomfortable. The cute innocence I knew of this girl was now guarded and on edge. After all, she was sitting in a maximum-security prison with a man she hadn't seen in years. I needed to turn on the charm and bring her back to a time and a boy she once knew.

While we were talking, I showed her a little crack on my back molar and said, "This is from the Christmas cookies you sent me while I was in Florida." She looked at me and started to laugh. I was smiling at her and flirting with her and all this managed to relax her. With her more comfortable, she managed to open up to me about her life and the things she had been through. She had a life I would've thought most women wished for, but I could tell she wasn't happy. She told me about her kids and how she was married. I could see the rock on her finger. She was well put together and taken care of, but I knew all too well happiness cannot be purchased.

I was listening to the words coming out of her mouth, but I was having trouble focusing because she was so beautiful. The little girl I remembered was now a grown woman with curves in all the right places. Every time she got up to go to the bathroom, I used those moments to gawk like a young boy. After I made her more comfortable, the conversation was great, but I could tell she was holding something back. When the officers announced they would be taking pictures I was excited. I wanted to take a picture with her because she was so

173

beautiful. She gave me a half-hearted argument I eventually won and we both received a picture together.

We had a great time on our visit, or at least I did. In or out of prison, it was always nice to hang out with this beautiful girl. The end of the visit came too fast and when it did, I gave her a hug and thanked her for coming to see me. She promised me she would come again. I was floating on a cloud when I left the visit. The feeling was so strong it didn't even bother me when I was strip searched by the officer on the way out.

I went to the prison yard and showed my photo to all my boys. In prison, it always feels good when someone cares enough to take the time out of their day to go through the hassle it takes to visit an inmate. That night, I couldn't stop thinking about her and fell asleep with her on my mind.

The next day I was having 3 people come visit me who were scheduled to speak with me about my affairs. In the morning, I got ready once again to go to the visit and I was called at 9am, the minute the visiting room opened. When I walked in, I was shocked as to who I saw. Once again, there was an angel sitting on the visit waiting for me. I checked in and made my way to the table she was sitting at and I looked at her and said, "What are you doing here?" She said, "I just needed to see you." Joy started nervously talking and I could feel she was getting all the heavy issues off her chest about her life and her problems. I was listening and trying to absorb everything she was saying. She wasn't happy, and it made me upset she wasn't happy. I had known this woman as a young girl, she was always a good girl. Why wasn't she happy?

I could tell she wanted something more out of life, I just didn't know what she wanted from me, so I said, "What do you want from me Joy?" She looked me in the eyes and said, "I can't stop thinking about you Jeff. I've loved you ever since I was a little girl and I have thought about you every single day, I even thought about you on my wedding day." I watched the tears start to swell in her eyes and she was upset when she said, "Why didn't you have sex with me in the Hamptons? I

174

was ready to give you my virginity! I need to know why you didn't want to have sex with me because this messed me up!"

I was in such a state of shock. I couldn't believe she thought I didn't "want" to have sex with her. Of course, I wanted to have sex with her! But I was a piece of shit and she deserved much better than me. I just sat there staring at her until she eventually looked away. I immediately said, "Look at me in my eyes and listen to me please. Joy, you were always my little baby and I believed wholeheartedly that you deserved your first experience to be with someone who was worthy of you. I cared about you, I wanted you to be with someone who was better than me because you were so special. You were supposed to marry a lawyer or doctor, not a piece of shit like me." She was looking at me with her big brown eyes and was stunned. I am guessing my explanation was one she never considered, but it was the truth.

When I was 15 years old, most people didn't see a teenage boy who was still trying to figure out life. The only one who ever saw me as just a boy was Joy. There was always something about her that made me deal with her differently. Joy had an innocence about her and her innocence caused me to be very overprotective of her. I cared about her in a way I didn't understand, and in a way, I couldn't put into words. My feelings for this sweet girl were confusing to me. She was a beautiful young girl, but I knew she deserved so much more than I could offer her. So, I just did my best to treat her special because at this point in my life, I wasn't capable of treating a girl the way a girl like Joy deserved to be treated. I wanted her to find someone who would treat her like a princess. I saw her differently than I did other girls and caring about her scared me. I had abandonment issues and in my eyes, I found it easiest to use girls. I didn't let anyone in and by me doing this, no one was able to hurt me. But she worked her way in and I had feelings for her. I couldn't fully act on these feelings because I didn't want to hurt her. I knew what kind of guy I was, and this beautiful young girl deserved more than I could have given her at this point in my life. I loved this girl, and this scared me.

I think Joy was still in a state of shock and I was in shock as well because this beautiful woman who was so good, better than a man like me deserved, just told me she loved me. I had plenty of girls tell me they loved me, but this was different, and she was different. When she told me this, it just seemed like this is how it was meant to be, this is how we were meant to be. My emotions were on overload and I was trying to just process everything that just happened and began to wonder, where do we go from here? I looked up and my other visitors were there. One of the visitors had to wait outside, because you're only allowed 3 adults visitors per visit, so Joy left. I believe by this point she was happy to escape because she just poured her heart and soul out to me and she was nervous. I was nervous as well because she was so special, and I was so unworthy.

I couldn't stop thinking about her. I was trying to focus on my visitors, but my mind was racing, and I couldn't stop replaying in my head what just happened. Not taking Joy's virginity was probably one of the only decent things I had ever done in my life, but me making the decision to not sleep with her, hurt her. It was never my intention to hurt her. The reason I didn't take her virginity was because I knew I would end up hurting her. I began to wonder what would have happened if I had taken her virginity. Could she have calmed me down? Probably not, but there is no way for us to ever know.

I didn't know what was going to happen between the two of us, but I knew I couldn't do what I had always done with other women. During this time, Joy separated from her husband and I had so many different girls writing me and visiting me. I immediately cut all of them off because I was already falling in love with Joy. I knew she was the one.

I was head over heels in love with her and our relationship grew. When she walked into a room, I was unable to see anyone but her. I had never been faithful to another woman, but with her it was different. She completed me. My fucked-up childhood caused me to suppress a lot of my issues because I lived in a world where I had to be tough and feared, but she had me open up to her. I had never done this with anyone before. I was a broken man, but she made me want to be better.

Joy was the only good thing in my life. She didn't love Jeff D the club kid, she didn't love Dutch Blood the gangster. She loved Jeff de Leyer, the young boy and young man she could still see the good in, even if no one else in the world could.

On a visit one day, Joy wasn't feeling too well. Her nose was stuffed up and red and she looked so cute, but she was miserable, and all she wanted to do was sleep. Joy rested her head on my shoulder and fell asleep in my arms. She had the front of her hair pulled up in a little clip thing and she looked like a sleeping angel. She would open her eyes on occasion and look at me and smile. I would kiss her on her forehead and watch as my pretty girl would drift back to sleep in my arms. I just sat silent and thought while I gently played with her hair. Here sat the love of my life but I was trapped in prison where I was unable to take care of her like she needed me to. This made me feel like a loser. I am the type of man who felt it was his job to provide for and to protect his woman. The harsh reality started to sink in. I had so much time left to do, and I would miss so much of our lives together. When I was with Joy, there was no other place in the world I would rather be. I was completely content with just watching her sleep in my arms. But the moment she would leave a visit, I was no longer content.

I was very caught up in my prison life and I was in some of the most notorious prisons in New York State. At the time, I was a young man with a lot of time on my hands and I was getting into a lot of trouble. I couldn't stay out of trouble. My boys were still very important to me and I was still young enough to be full of bad decisions. I couldn't stay in a prison for long, because I was starting a lot of problems. It takes a special kind of trouble to get kicked out of Maximum Security Prisons.

In prison, there are unwritten rules that are dictated mostly behind a man's pride and a perceived honor that only exists in the penitentiary. At the time, I was still selling drugs with the little homies. In the drug game in prison, a man cannot take any shorts (loses) or he will be perceived as weak. Men in prison are constantly trying to get over on each other. I had negotiated a deal with a Rat Hunter (Rat Hunter is a prison gang) for $50 cash money for some marijuana. When I handed the guy the product, he handed me something that I perceived to be the $50 rolled up. In prison, we roll the money up because it is easier to hide. What this inmate had done was cut the corner of a $50 bill and folded it the same way as if it was the cash. When I unrolled what I thought was the $50 there was a short missive that said, "You have two options. You can either hold it down or we can go gun to gun." What this meant was, I could take the loss, or we could fight with knives. I chose the latter.

The day before the administration had swept the yard with metal detectors, removing all the hidden knives. Because I had been so comfortable, I was outside without a weapon. The Rat Hunter who had tried to get over was standing with four or five of his boys across the yard. He lifted his shirt, so I could see the knife. I told one of the little homies to go and find me a weapon. A minute later, the little homie appeared with two blades that had come out of a shaving razor. I told the little homie I would be better off using my hand.

As the group of Rat Hunters started to make their way across the yard towards me, I said, "Make sure no one gets behind me." I watched him pull the knife from his waistband and hold it in an underhand grip with his right hand. I knew all I had to do was control the hand the knife was in and I would be alright. When my assailant got within arm's reach, I allowed him to swing once and I caught his wrist. With his wrist secure, I fought him hockey style and I used my right hand to beat him until I heard the knife hit the ground.

At this point, the officer in the tower started screaming for us to break it up. Out of the corner of my eye, I noticed other officers responding to the area, so I pulled my red hoodie off and slipped into the crowd that was gathered under the sports TV. This caused the officers to chase the wrong inmates. Shortly thereafter, they made an announcement on the loud speaker stating they were running early go back from the yard, and I slipped into the group going back to the cellblock. In my cell, I spent the night contemplating what needed to be done. I did not want to get kicked out of Greenhaven because it was closer for Joy. However, prison policy required I finish what this man started.

I worked in the medical unit at the prison. When I went to work early in the morning I called Joy to let her know what was going on. Of course, I played down the seriousness of the situation, so I wouldn't upset her. I explained that I was going to hit someone. She was upset and begged me not to do anything. She didn't understand how prison is. I used to tell her all the time that this wasn't the Boys Club or the Boy Scouts, that this was Maximum Security Prison. Looking back, I don't think she ever truly understood how dangerous prison really is. The only experience she had with prison was the visiting room. The visiting room is filled with wives and children, family and friends. She didn't understand the visiting room was nothing like the yard. The two cannot even be compared.

Later that evening, I strapped two magazines, one in the front, and one in the back, and secured them with a weight belt around my stomach. I tied my hoodie tight, put my brown leather gloves in my back pocket, removed the knife I had hidden behind my toilet and went to the yard to handle my business.

The minute I stepped in the yard it was as if the whole population had taken a deep breath. The tension was so thick, it could have been cut with a knife. I have never been one for talking when shit is about to pop of. I told one of the old timers who I had known since I was a kid, to go and arrange for me and the kid to go gun to gun behind the handball court. With the fight set up, I took two of the little homies and the old timer with me to the handball court to hold me down. The little homie tried to hand me a prison made mace bottle, but I was cocky and considering I beat this man up the day before without a weapon, I declined. Prison mace consists of bleach and jalapeno juice. This is used to spray in prisoner's eyes.

After the officers had made their rounds and could not see us, me and my opponent squared off. When he rushed at me, I stabbed him in the mid-section and felt the knife sink in. He jumped back, reached into his hoodie and pulled out his own mace. He sprayed a thick stream into my eyes and my instinct was to rub my eyes, which caused the bleach and jalapeno juice to blind me. Not being able to see distracted me as I felt a hard-painful blow to my left eye. I swung my knife frantically, at nothing but air. The homies were chanting me on, "Get em, get em Dutch" not realizing I was unable to see. Had my assailant been more ruthless, he could have taken my life. Feeling secure in what he had done, he started talking shit as he left.

The homies brought me to a table and tried to help me flush out my eyes. The old timer, had taken Vaseline out of his shower bag and packed the hole in my face. The game plan was for me to make it back inside and flush my eyes out, so I could see, and then stab one of the Rat Hunters in front of the officers and get shipped out of the prison. The old timer locked in a different cell block from me and the little homies. The Rat Hunter waited until the old timer left my side and two of the top Rat Hunters came in one direction, while they sent the actual assailants to sneak us from the back. I was nervous because all I could see were blurs.

The homie that was standing behind me was stabbed in the neck and fell. Out of pure fright, I turned around and swung and connected with my assailant before he could stab me. I just kept swinging until he ran off. The little homie was laid out right behind me. One of the men I worked with grabbed me by the arm and escorted me to the corner. He said, "You alright Dutch?" I said, "Just let me know if any Spanish dudes come my way." The officers opened the door and dragged the little homie inside. The cops didn't care, they wanted to continue running the early go back.

At this point I still couldn't see, but I knew I needed to make it past the checkpoint in the hallway that would lead me into the cellblock. All the little homies had dispersed right after the second attack, so I was alone and afraid because I couldn't see, but my spider senses were on high alert. I managed to pass the officer at the checkpoint and I used my hand to feel the wall. I walked down the hallway towards the cell block, until one of the little homies made his way to my side and helped get me back to my cell. The men who locked on my company helped me clean up as best as possible. I spent the whole night getting ready for the kamikaze mission I was planning to get me to the box (solitary confinement) safely.

Bright and early in the morning, I heard the inmate in the first cell scream down the company, "Walking". This is a sign to alert the prisoners to the presence of officers. I turned the side of my face to the wall, but the officer was headed to my cell. When he got in front of my cell, he cracked the door open and said, "Hey asshole, how long did you think you were going to sit with that hole in your face? We got about 20 kites (notes) telling us you were stabbed in the yard last night." Even though it was obvious what had happened, I pleaded the fifth.

I was then handcuffed and taken to the prison hospital where the doctors determined I would need to be taken to the outside hospital. The closest hospital that handled prisoners was Westchester Medical. In the emergency room of Westchester Medical, the female doctor stated that due to me sitting in my cell all night, they could no longer stitch up the hole in my face. From there, I was brought to the Ophthalmologist who deemed the bleach had burnt out my tear ducts. I was brought back to Greenhaven's inmate hospital where I was placed in hospital segregation.

The little homie who was stabbed, was in the room next to me. The lieutenant investigating the incident, came into my room and asked me once again what had happened, and I stayed silent. The code of prison mandates that no inmate should ever tell the cops anything. The lieutenant had pitched different scenarios to me. He said, "That little homie in the next room stabbed you and then you stabbed him over drug deals. I have two years of tape of you and the little homie smoking marijuana together." I said, "If you have tape of us smoking, it is obvious we are friends. How is he doing? It was his birthday yesterday." The lieutenant said, "He is lucky to be alive. He keeps complaining he is cold in there." I had two thermal shirts on when they had taken me to the hospital. I pulled one of the shirts off my back and said, "Can you give this to him?" I believed this simple gesture convinced him we didn't stab each other.

The little homie was eventually taken to IPC (Involuntary Protective Custody) and the day after, I was taken to IPC. I had a pending ticket, so I was locked in my cell. The little homie who could barely move his neck, pulled up a chair in front of my cell and said, "Dutch, I fucking hate you for getting me stabbed on my birthday." Going through an experience like this made our bond that much stronger. The little homie leaned in and said, "What the fuck are the cops doing?" Because I was in the cell and could not see, I took my mirror and stuck it out of the cell bars, so I could see where the officers were at. I observed the officers sneaking around the corner to spy on our conversation. At this point, they were still not sure if we were enemies. Once they had determined we were not enemies and they weren't going to see a fight, they had locked him up as well. Every time the administration walked on the unit, I would hand over a bowl of food to the little homie and I would tell him in a loud joking manner, it was poisoned. I thought this was funny, but the administration did not.

While all of this was going on, I was unable to use the phone. I had one of the little homies call Joy and explain that I had been hit, but I was fine, and I loved her. The next day I was told I had a visit. I walked into the visiting room and there she was waiting for me. Joy took one look at my eye and she immediately burst into tears. Not knowing prison lingo, Joy assumed "hit" meant I had been punched in the face. I spent the entire six-hour visit reassuring her how I was fine while she just cried. I looked in her eyes and saw her fear. This made me feel like shit because I could deal with the repercussions of my life in prison, but she shouldn't have had to. I could truly see how my life was affecting the woman I loved.

* * * * * *

I spent the next four months going back and forth to the ophthalmologist. The mace had done more damage than the knife had. I eventually was transferred out of the facility and sent to Sing Sing Correctional Facility and as usual, I couldn't manage to keep myself out of trouble. Once I arrived at Sing Sing, I had a chip on my shoulder and felt like I needed to get revenge.

For the next 8 months, I would personally assault or order the assault of any Rat Hunter who had come from Greenhaven to Sing Sing. I ordered the assault of one Rat Hunter which ended up causing a riot between the Spanish dudes and Bloods in the B-Block Gym. The Latin Kings would fight against the other Spanish gangs, but when it was time to bang out against the Bloods, the Spanish gangs would all unify. I did not witness the riot due to medical calling me to the dentist. This same night, we were let out into the yard and I cut one of the Spanish gang leaders and got away.

In the morning, I was snatched up and brought to Administrative Segregation, and from there I was shipped out of the facility. The administration was trying to pin the assault of 11 Spanish Inmates on me, even though I wasn't present during the riot because I was at the dentist. The Administration was unable to prove I was the cause of the riot, but they felt as though they didn't need to prove it. All they needed to do was claim I was a threat to the safety and security of the building and just like that, I was in Ad-Seg.

Joy had different tactics to try to get me to behave. She drew up a little contract stating how I needed to be good and stay out of trouble, and it had all sorts of cute threats in it. The contract stated, if I didn't get myself together and stay out of trouble, I was going to lose her. She made me sign the contract and return it to her. I laughed her cute little contract off because I was too stupid to see the signs. I loved her in the only way I was capable of loving her, but I truly didn't know how to love her in the way she needed. One day we were on a visit and when Joy went to the lady's room, I ran over to speak to one of the little homies. One of the Correctional Officers thought he overheard me hand down an order to this other inmate and after I left the visit, I was immediately shipped to the furthest prison in NY State, Clinton Correctional Facility.

As soon as I arrived at Clinton, they took me to the id room to receive my prison identification. Once they realized who I was, I was immediately placed on Unit 14. Unit 14 was a unit that housed inmates on death row in NY state. The New York Court of Appeals eventually declared the death penalty unconstitutional and in 2007, the last remaining death sentences were reduced to natural life. New York State was now left with a vacant death row, and I was eventually placed in segregation in another part of the prison.

* * * * * *

We had been together for 4 years while I was in Clinton Correctional facility. Clinton is located on the border of Canada and was 10 hours away from Joy. The distance made things difficult. Joy was such a good girl, but she was also very naïve to prison. I guess you could say I tried to turn her into someone she wasn't, because I expected her to just accept my life in prison.

Most men in prison who are gang affiliated, have wives or girlfriends who were raised in the hood. These women understood the game and understood prison life. Joy was the complete opposite from most of the little homies wives or girlfriends. Joy was a very intelligent woman, but she lacked street smarts. There was nothing "hood" about her. She lived a very sheltered life and I let her know too much because I never wanted to lie to her, yet I didn't even notice I was pushing her away. When Joy and I were together or on the phone, there was no question if we were in love. However, the sad truth of life is, sometimes love isn't enough.

When I was brought down to the visit I was handcuffed and shackled. She saw my get up before the officers could get my animal chains off and she started crying. It hurt me to see her cry, but I was happy to see the love of my life. She was there to reveal some news, news I never saw coming. I leaned in and gave Joy a kiss and I could tell that there was something on her mind. I said, "What's wrong pretty girl?" She said, "I need to tell you something." I looked into her eyes and said, "Ok, tell me." Joy said, "I met a man and he took me out on a date." I was instantly devastated, but being me, I tried my best to not reveal how hurt I really was. I said, "Did you sleep with him?" She said,

"No". I said, "Did you kiss him?" She said, "No". I wanted to believe her and trust her because this woman was the love of my life. She started to cry, and she said, "I am so sorry baby, it will never happen again." And I believed her.

We spent the rest of the visit trying to pretend what she had told me was not such a big deal. However, when I went back to my cell I was crushed. I did not want to lose this woman, and I couldn't believe she would betray me. I didn't know what to do so I tried to put it in the back of my head where I had learned to store everything that had ever bothered me in my entire life. This was a coping mechanism I had learned as a child. Little did I know, one day all the demons I locked away would rear their ugly heads and haunt me to the point of almost losing my mind.

I trusted her with my heart and I understood her life was difficult. She was a beautiful woman, men wanted, but I never thought I would lose her. We talked on the phone, but she didn't come see me anymore. One day while we were on the phone she told me I should marry one of the boys in prison because I always chose them over her. This killed me. And one day her phone was cut off. I wrote letters that never received answers and I finally realized she was gone. I was destroyed. I had finally known love and it was stripped away from me. To lose her, made me even wilder.

I became extremely violent and I took out my pain on the men I was getting into confrontations with. Prison is full of men who are looking for a problem, and I made sure I had what they were looking for. I was angry, and I didn't care if I lived or died. This was a very dangerous mix. I didn't let any girls other than family and friends come visit me for over 4 years. I waited for her, hoping she would come back, but she didn't.

THIRTEEN

ISOLATION

"The hardest prison to escape is in your mind" -*Unknown*

Solitary confinement is inevitable at some point for prisoners who are serving a long-term sentence. For gang members, the box is a given because it's a favored disciplinary strategy of the department of corrections. Currently, there are all sorts of studies of the negative effects of locking a human in a cell with next to nothing for long periods of time.

The box is about repetitive days. One day is no different than another. A man gets up in the morning and is served breakfast at 7am, after breakfast is served, he may be handcuffed and escorted outside to a cage where he is entitled to one hour of fresh air. Once the hour is up, the inmate is returned to the box. Lunch arrives at around 11am. The next major event is mail call at 3:30 where every box inmate hopes somebody will have remembered him and then dinner is served by 4:30.

I have done a lot of time in Solitary Confinement and it takes a strong mind to make it through the box. I have been locked in the box with only my demons to keep me company. I have not met a man who has done any box time who has not thought of killing himself. I have witnessed several dead bodies being pulled out of solitary confinement cells.

The first time I went to the box after losing Joy, I was in a dark place already. I received 270 days of box time for an assault charge. I felt alone in population when I was surrounded by hundreds of people and now I was in a cell where the lights were never turned off. The mail man passed my cell every day without a letter. The stench of piss and shit was the natural smell of the unit. I was starving, because the three small meals I was fed, just wasn't enough and there are no commissary purchases allowed in the box. In the middle of the night, it wasn't unusual to hear men talking to themselves or crying themselves to sleep. You are allowed 10 personal photos in the box, and I had taken photos of Joy with me. The pictures didn't help my mood though, they actually made me feel worse.

I used to lay on my bed and just stare at the ceiling. I would think about how I allowed the love of my life to slip away, think about how I fucked up my life. You must realize, when you are in the box, you are in jail, inside of jail. I spent my days having thoughts and memories flash through my head. My grandmother, suddenly dying, not living long enough to see me free. The woman I loved, laughing, crying, telling me she loved me, her voice, her eyes, our visits, phone calls, thoughts of us when we were young, her hair, men, around her, touching her, death, fear, sadness, hurt, sick, telling another man she loves him, she's gone, she left, she lied, she cheated, thoughts of her having sex with another man, her smile, smiling at me, smiling at him, my woman, his woman, I love her, how, why, anger, pain, rage, uncontrollable rage.

My flash thoughts were like demons and they would chase me. There have been occasions where I would pace and talk to myself just to hear a voice in an attempt to escape the flash thoughts. I had spent many days pushing the line of insanity. With nothing to take your mind off your troubles, they build up and get worse with every slow second that passes, until you pray and hope you fall asleep.

This time I spent nine months in the box and by the time I got out, I was 25lbs lighter. I did not get one visit and only received a handful of letters from my family. My next box trip was much longer.

I cut a Crip and I felt someone grab me so my instinct led me to turn around and swing. I had not realized the person who grabbed me was an officer. Once I delivered the blow, the repercussions were inevitable. I was beat unconscious by the C.O.'s and dragged into the box. I awoke to hearing the homies scream my name, "Dutch, Dutch, you alright?" I rose from the floor, battered and bruised and went to the door and said, "I'm alive." Because of the common brutality of the officers in Attica, escaping with my life was something to be grateful for. They had knocked 3 teeth out of my mouth, bruised and battered my body, but normally, most inmates end up much worse. After being sentenced to 30 months, I was transported to Southport Correctional Facility. Southport is the max box in NY State.

How can I get you to understand Solitary Confinement? Go grab one pen, a pad of paper and 10 photos and walk into a closet and shut the door. You may last an hour or two and this is with the knowledge you can just get up and walk out. Now try to imagine being locked in that very closet knowing you had months or quite possibly years before you would be let out. This is the easiest way to describe the box, but your closet is no comparison. You can't hear the screams of grown men all day and night long, you can't smell the stink of piss and shit. Some men go bat shit crazy. I have known men for years who appeared normal, but lost their minds in the box. How long do you think you could last?

There are different levels of the box. Level One, you are not allowed anything extra. Level Two, you are allowed one pair of personal shorts, one pair of personal sneakers, 10 extra photos and 5 extra books. If you do not possess these things, you don't get anything. You are also allowed one pair of headphones to plug in the wall so you can listen to either music or programs. If you catch a ticket, you are sent back to Level One to start over again.

Upon me entering Level One at Southport I was placed inside my cell and after I dropped my belongings on the bed, I knocked on the wall and said, "What's your handle". In a gruff growl, he said, "Around these parts, they call me the shit general." In the box, you have inmates who think of their feces as chemical warfare. They will piss and shit in containers and let it marinate in their cell until they deem it is worth throwing, spitting or slinging at whoever they have problems with. Usually, these box terrorists never leave the box and go back to population, because the antics they use as warfare, have them marked for a life of retaliation. Instigating one of these box terrorists may be as simple as denying him a magazine.

With the shit general being my neighbor, I was not about to allow him to fling shit at me after I got out of the shower. Since his cell was located closer to the shower than mine, I decided him and I would be friends. I said, "Do you drink coffee?" He said, "Yeah, I drink coffee." I said, "I get a kosher meal and I don't like coffee so you can have my decaffeinated Sanka's every morning." I was one of the lucky ones who would make it to Level Two, before the shit general and I could have a falling out. Men like the shit general, rarely make it out of Level One.

* * * * * *

I spent the next couple of years in and out of solitary confinement. After my first trip without Joy, I became numb to the feelings that would attack me in the cell. I had built up a protective layer with the assistance of heavy drug use, which allowed me not to care. I started feeling like there wasn't anything else they could do to me. I just didn't give a fuck anymore.

My mother knew how depressed I was after losing Joy so she decided to bring Grandma up to visit me. Grandma just had surgery and being the stubborn Dutch woman she was, refused to use a cane. I came down to the visit so excited to see my Grandmother and mother. While on the visit, I had to escort Grandma to and from anywhere she went. It made me sad to see that her body was giving up on her because she was always my idea of strength.

After eating lunch on the visit, I was speaking to my mother about the day to day prison life and everything I was going through. Not being conscious of the words that were coming out of my mouth, I was using excessive profanity. Grandma may not have been able to walk as well as she used to, but she still had a mean right hook which I experienced as she said, "Watch your mouth." The guard who knew me looked at the table when he heard the crack of grandma's hand connecting with my face. The look that I gave him let him know that if he came over to my table and said anything to my grandmother, there would be problems. I could tell by the smirk on his face, he was happy to see at least someone knew how to discipline me. So, he let the infraction ride. This was the last time I ever saw my Grandmother.

The loss of Joy continued to torture me. I did not know if I would be able to find happiness with another woman. Yet after so many years, I felt that I deserved to at least try. I decided to write her a letter with one last hope she would come to her senses and come back to me. I needed to write her one last time, before I could even attempt to allow another woman to come visit me. The fact that Joy never gave me any form of closure, haunted me every single day she was gone. It's difficult to accept you did something wrong, when you had no idea what you did wrong.

Dear Joy,

I don't even know if you even still live here, but it ain't shit but 41 cents and a little of my time. I just want you to know not a day goes by I don't think about you. You know that you're still the love of my life and I understand that the life I live is a lot to deal with. I just hope the man in your life treats you as you deserve.

As for myself, I'm more or less on my own. You fucked me up because I had everything I needed and wanted in you, so I guess I'm just going to ride it out. I got my boys so I'll be alright, plus my son who is like my brother just got home so he has been in my corner. But you know I'm lonely because even though I have a support group, I don't have you. It's like I lost half of my soul.

This is the story of my life now. Do you see what I was telling you when you first came through? I've known my whole life that the only one I can count on is me. Not that you didn't want to, but my life is too real. I'm not a husband, I am everything you don't need. You have men that die in their beds, surrounded by loved ones. Me, I'm destined to die at the hands of violence and at this point, I am alright with this.

The way shit works out is crazy. After you abandoned me I was fucked up, depressed, mad and confused but after the smoke cleared out of my mind, I had to be realistic and just be glad for the time I did get from you. And if I ever make it out of the pen, you can bet you'll see me because one day you will have to look me in the eyes and tell me you don't love me. And if god forbid I get killed in one of these yards, maybe I'll be able to look into your soul and find the answers I need.

Listen I'm going to keep this short, but if you choose you know how to find me. Stay up and stay safe.

The One and Only,
Dutch

I waited every day for her to respond, but the letter never came. It was so difficult to accept it was over. I spent years wondering if what we had was ever real. The truth of her situation would have killed me had I found out then.

After time, I tried to replace her. I would get plugged into a girl who was interested in me and I would find a reason not to like them. I even got back together with Rachael, my childhood girlfriend after she wrote me a random letter.

Rachael had been in and out of my life since I was 12 years old. The problem was, the problems we had in the beginning would continue to resurface. Rachel and I did not trust each other and we both liked to constantly bring up the past. Rachel and I had an on and off relationship for years which consisted of us both cheating. In Rachael's letter, she told me how sorry she was for not being strong enough to be the woman I needed in prison, and how she had grown up so much and was finally ready to do what needed to be done. She eventually came to visit me and I knew right from the moment I saw her, this wasn't going to work because I was still so in love with Joy. Rachel tried to convince me that what we had was love but I knew it wasn't. I experienced love with Joy and this was not it. But, I was tired of being by myself so I kept up with the charade that was our relationship. It was so bad, Racheal would question my level of attraction to her because she sensed something was wrong.

I contemplated marrying this woman just because I did not want to be alone. I felt like I was getting older and I should be married. Rachael would visit me frequently and bring me the things I needed behind the walls of prison. This allowed me to deal with the fact that I was settling with her. Our visits were robotic, we were just going through the motions. I believed Rachel was more in love with being the wife of Jeff de Leyer, than being with me. I was relieved when it was finally over. If I were to get married one day, I wanted it to be forever. I knew with Rachael it would never be forever.

When Joy was away, I had a lot of time to reflect and her leaving me caused me to seek change in my life. I couldn't keep doing the same things and expect different outcomes. At least not good ones. I was starting to realize the laws of Karma and how they would affect my life.

FOURTEEN

WELCOME TO BARD

"Art washes away from the soul, the dust of everyday life"
-Pablo Picasso

O ut of pure luck, I was transferred to Eastern Correctional Facility. Eastern is a prison with a lot of great programs and the prison is the least violent of all the New York Maximum Security Prisons. In this new environment, I was able to start working on myself. In this new prison, the most popular inmates weren't the most violent inmates. The popular inmates were the ones who accomplished great academic achievements in the college program, or possessed outstanding athletic abilities in the many sports programs provided by this facility. They had theater programs, music programs, all sorts of programs to keep you busy and focused. Eastern made me want more. Eastern made me want to go to college.

I was getting visits but I missed Joy so much and I couldn't have a successful relationship, because I was in love with a woman who was only in my life as a memory. One of my old Graf buddies Russia transferred into the prison. Russia was one of the BTS boys and he was a really good artist. In the streets he was good with his cans, but in prison he learned to use brushes. I needed something to be passionate about. Russia gave me a starter set of paint and brushes, and I started playing around with them that very night. My first piece was a graffiti piece. I was excited to show Russia my completed project in the morning. Russia looked at it and said, "We already know you know how to do graffiti, paint something else." I was determined to prove I could do something else.

I remembered watching the Bob Ross painting show and I decided to try and recreate a scenery. Armed with my paintbrush and my cheap set of paints, I went back into my cell and tried to create a forest. I managed to pull off certain parts, but others not so much. When I was done, I believed I had created something beautiful and I was so proud of myself. I rushed to show Russia and the other guys what I had done. This small accomplishment had inspired me to believe I could paint. I finally found something I could be passionate about. I spent hours practicing. I was reading books about techniques and artists themselves. The better I got, the more critical of my work I became. When I sucked, I thought I was great, and when I was good, I realized I had a lot of work ahead of me to become great. I have always had a good work ethic and because I didn't possess extraordinary talent, I worked harder.

Eastern has a college program that is part of the Bard College. One hundred and fifty men every year write an essay and try to get accepted. To get into this program, essays are turned over to a panel of professors who pick 45 of the most interesting submissions. If your submission is chosen, you are granted an in-person interview. Out of those 45 applicants, only 15 are granted admission. The first time I applied and wrote my essay, I wrote an essay that my preconceived notion led me to believe this was what the liberal college wanted to hear. I didn't get in or even called for an interview. I was upset because I thought I was smart.

I got involved with other programs because I needed to stay busy and my outlook on life started to change. I was painting and drawing every day. This allowed me to clear my head and really think about what I wanted and who I wanted to be. I wanted to be more than a gang member or notorious criminal. I was part of a yoga class, I helped teach a public speaking class and me and a couple of other artists started a drawing class. These programs helped me to realize I could be more than I believed I could be.

When the signup sheet came out for the essay application I decided I would try again. When I sat down in the school building to write my essay, I decided this essay would be written my way and if it wasn't chosen, at least I had written what I wanted to write. You had to choose one of three different topics to write about. I decided my essay would be about the blind faith of American Soldiers. The essay was raw, but I had insight about following a cause. When I was recruited into the Bloods, I was fed a lot of propaganda that I believed and I followed orders. When I turned my essay in I felt good.

To find out who would be granted an interview took about a month. The first time I wrote my essay I was stressing the entire wait. The second go around I didn't even think about it. No man in my family had ever been to college, so if I didn't make it, maybe college wasn't for me. When the interview list came out, I was the third name on the list. I was reading a book about Hieronymus Bosch at the time of the interview.

I walked into the classroom that Max and Dan (the Bard Administration) were holding the interviews in and introduced myself. We talked for a while and I steer the conversation onto the subject of art. Dan was well versed on Bosch and we discussed a few ideas about the mockery of the religion that was his patron for his work. After this conversation, Dan said, "What do you know about Pablo Picasso?" I said, "I knew Pablo Picasso was not the creator of his cubism style, but currently, I do not have enough information to present good arguments." Dan looked at me and said, "Soon enough you will." I took this as a good sign and I was so excited when I left the interview. I was accepted into college two weeks later.

I was lonely and thought of Joy often. Rachael had tried to come back into my life again during this time, but it couldn't work because my heart belonged to Joy. Thinking of her was a mixed bag of emotions. I loved her, she taught me how to feel and love, but she didn't believe in me or us. I knew I did things that pushed her away because I was stupid and selfish. I had left so many of my true feelings on the table unsaid. I spent so many nights staring at the ceiling thinking about her and it hurt. I couldn't be happy without her. I knew she would have be proud of me for getting into college, but she wasn't around for me to tell her.

College was a new experience for me. I had left the streets in 1998 and came to prison. In Eastern, there is a school building located on the second floor across from the mess hall where there are classrooms, a computer lab and a library for inmates who were part of the Bard College Program. I was not a computer guy and all my papers had to be typed. On a good day, I may be able to type 35-40 words per minute. I would lose my papers and had to ask one of the guys to find them. They would end up in my music and all sorts of places they shouldn't be. I worked my ass off while expanding my mind with the books I was reading. I was also inspiring new ideas for my paintings.

* * * * * *

One day I was painting in my cell when the Chaplin called me into his office to tell me my Grandmother had passed. Grandma had gotten sick at the very end of her life. I had been told to prepare for this, but it still destroyed me and I broke down. My family made the necessary arrangements with the prison to bring me down for the wake. All I could think about was the last time Grandma saw me was on a visit in prison. I felt like such a disappointment to her. I wasn't there for my Grandmother due to my poor choices and she was one of the only people who had always been there for me.

I stayed silent for the ride down. The officers who brought me knew me and tried to brighten my spirits, but I was really feeling the burden of my life choices. I had caused someone else's family to deal with the same tremendous loss I was now feeling, and their loss had someone to blame. That someone was me. I spent the entire drive down replaying memories of my Grandmother. I couldn't believe I would never see her again.

When the van pulled up to the funeral home, everything started to sink in. I was trying to be strong but it was difficult. I was about to see family members I hadn't seen in years and they would have to see me like an animal. I wasn't allowed into the funeral home until my family arrived, so we sat in the van and waited. A few minutes later, I saw a white truck pull up and watched as my mother, cousins and sister exited and made their way inside.

I was led into the funeral home by the officers handcuffed and shackled, and the first person I saw was my mother. The handcuffs didn't allow me to hug anyone, but my mother hugged me and she was crying. When she walked away, I looked ahead and found myself instantly drawn to the casket. It was as though I was being pulled. I didn't want to look inside but I did and fell to my knees. I felt my eyes moisten and two tears slid down my face. I was crushed because my fucked-up choices caused people who loved me to suffer. That's the thing about being selfish, sometimes it's too late to be sorry and it hurts to realize this.

I spoke and attempted to console my family. My Aunt Chris used my handcuffs and shackles as a warning to her boys as she pointed to me and said, "See, this is what happens when boys don't listen and when they misbehave." My cousins who were little children when I went away, where now young men and women. My sister Heather was there. She flew up from Florida with my father. My father looked old and tired and I became very nervous about his health. My father had not been in my life like I may have needed him, but I now understood as a man, leaving me with Harriet was his way of trying to do right by me.

There were two shining moments I would like to believe my Grandmother's spirit played a part in. My sisters went and picked up my daughter Alexis who was 17 years old so I could see her. The last time I saw Alexis, she was four years old. I hugged and kissed her as best as I could in my chains as I told her, "I am so sorry. I need you to know that there has not been a day that has passed, when you weren't on my mind." My daughter was another victim of my bad choices because I wasn't around to be the father she needed. I wasn't man enough in the streets to be her Dad. Matt's sister Rachel had brought her two kids so I could see them in person. She had sent me pictures, but this was the first time I was ever able to meet them. I felt like my Grandmother was reminding me I had something to live for and people who wanted me to come home.

As I was escorted into the back of the van to be returned to my cage, I saw the faces of people who loved me even though I had spent years feeling like no one cared. The tears just started to flow and I didn't try to stop them. I was just hoping they would release some of the pain. When I arrived back to the prison, I painted for the next couple of days. I only took breaks for food and sleep. Painting for me, had the ability to allow me to process and attempt to deal with my thoughts. The juvenile me would have wanted someone else to feel my pain, but I was trying to put this boy to rest.

* * * * * *

Shortly after my Grandmother's funeral my daughter had turned 18 years old and she was able to come visit me. I had missed all her life because of my poor choices. What men who run the streets fail to understand, our choices are subject to affect our children, our loved ones and anyone else who may need us in their lives. I had lost the love of my life, but I had a daughter to catch up with whose mother had kept me away for the most part. I was broken after losing Joy and I was about to receive another shot.

My daughter wanted to go on a family reunion visit with me, but we needed to go and straighten out her Birth Certificate, due to choices her mother made when she was born. After we petitioned the family court for the change, we needed to take a DNA test. As far as I was concerned, this was all just going through the motions. My daughter looked like my sisters and had a lot of my traits.

A few weeks later, the family court held our hearing and I was rocked when the test came back that Alexis wasn't my child. I had thought of this little girl for all her life. Grandma had grabbed her and declared her a de Leyer baby, so no matter what a stick rubbed in my mouth said, Alexis was still my daughter. But it hurt, and I broke down. Once upon a time I was numb to my emotions and feelings, but Joy had made me open up when we were together and when you start opening up, you become susceptible to pain. I was now feeling pain and I just couldn't deal. I had lost the love of my life, my freedom, my youth, my grandmother and now this. I ended up going back to what kept the pain away –drugs.

Prisons are flooded with drugs and I was a Gang Member, so drugs were always around and I started getting high again. The drugs didn't make anything better, they just allowed me not to give a shit about anything. I was painting on all night benders; my work was good but my life was becoming more messed up. I ended up in solitary confinement on a drug related charge that got me shipped out of Eastern and because of this, out of my college program.

After my solitary confinement time was up, I ended up staying in solitary for an extra four weeks. Because of all the trouble I had gotten into, it is difficult to find a prison to place me in. The administration does not want too many high-profile inmates all in one prison. I had changed a lot while in Eastern, but I was broken. Joy had been gone for over 8 years and I just couldn't deal with the way she would consume my thoughts.

On Father's Day, I was called at 9:30 am to the visit. This was not a scheduled visit so I got ready as quickly as possible and headed to the visit room floor. When I walked into the room, I saw Rachael on the visit with my friend which caused me to scan the visiting room, to see who had called me on the visit. I saw my daughter.

This was the first visit since we found out she wasn't biologically mine. I checked in at the desk quickly, and made my way back to our table. The visit room was packed with people wanting to spend time with their incarcerated fathers. It made me feel good that Alexis and my relationship was still strong. I gave her a hug and we sat down and I said, "Regardless of what a DNA test stated, Grandma said you were mine, and this holds more weight than any DNA test ever could." She said, "Don't worry, I am not going anywhere and you are still my father." The fucked-up thing in this poor girls' life was, I was the steadiest father figure she had, and I was gone for 14 years.

We talked back and forth and fell right into our usual banter. When they opened the outside visit room, we went outside so we could sit at a table with Rachael and my friend. We sat talking about Long Island and the three of them were telling me about the things I had missed. My friend had only been in jail for a year, and Alexis and Rachael lived in the same general area. We were trying to figure out where Alexis was going to live, because she wasn't living with her mother anymore and she was no longer living with her aunt. She wanted to be on her own, but she was not financially ready. The day went off without a hitch, yet it would be the last time I saw her.

We continued to speak but with each phone call, the time between them got longer. Not from a lack of me trying, but from Alexis slowly pushing away. I would write her letters, telling her regardless of what happens, she will always be able to count on me, but I needed to give her the space that she needed. She eventually moved down south and I never heard from her again. Shortly thereafter, I was shipped out of Eastern and placed in Auburn Correctional Facility. I was now back in a war zone.

* * * * * *

Auburn is the second oldest prison in the United States and it is the oldest prison that still houses inmates. Auburn is also the most violent prison in New York State. The presence of death can be felt as soon as you enter the prison. I had gone from the least violent prison to the most violent and it was time to readjust. I am a survivor and I do what I have to do.

I was trying to change for the better, yet I was caught between the old me, Dutch Blood and the man I wanted to be, Dutch the artist. I was conflicted because I was questioning if I could be more than a Gangster. After all, the woman who was supposed to love me since she was 14 years old, didn't believe in me. People loved my paintings, but I couldn't sell my work due to being in prison so I had to sell drugs in prison in order to feed myself. When I tried to do right, no one helped me, but if I was scheming on illegal money, people believed in my plans and helped. This fact made me question if I was just meant to be nothing more than I was. It's hard to believe in yourself when no one else does, but at this time I was so passionate about art, I had to continue to work. Art allowed me to have a voice and escape through my visual images.

It was difficult to stay focused in Auburn because my old reputation followed me and I was still being active in the gang life. I was involved in two riots and managed to get away, but every day was possibly my last day in population because the administration knew who I was and with them, I was still the same dude I'd always been. Auburn has a college program that is part of Cornell College. I was taking classes, but Auburn was not conducive to the productive betterment of an inmate. I was using drugs every day to numb the pain of my reality and was still getting A's in the courses I was taking. The workload wasn't like it was in the Bard program. I was really trying to get back to Eastern and my transfer was in. I was waiting to be transferred but I had to stay out of trouble. As usual, this wasn't possible for me.

Prison Riots are scary because it is a free for all of violence and mayhem. Because of the strong gang presence in prison and the fact that gang members are obligated to fight for their brothers, it is easy for something small to create a big problem.

In October of 2013 a semi-high-ranking Blood had been released from solitary confinement after several years of being locked down. In Auburn, each different gang or organization had phones in the yard they considered theirs for only their people to use. To use a phone without being given permission by the men who are holding that phone down is considered a violation. If a group lets others move in on their phone without a show of strength, that group will lose the phone. The crazy thing is, if two guys stab each other over the phone, neither one of them will be using the phone in solitary confinement. Yet, this is how it is.

The Blood kid didn't know how the phones were setup in Auburn nor did he seem to care. The Homie came into the yard and got on the first phone he saw. The phone was a Black Lions phone. The Black Lions are a Jamaican gang. The Lion approached the Homie and he was respectful knowing the homie was a new face. The Lion said, "Rude boy, this is a Lion phone and when you done, make sure you give the phone back to the people." The Homie looked at the Lion and said, "Yeah, whatever son" with a dismissive tone. The Lion posted up in front of phone which was in the main yard, and when the homie hung the phone up, the Lion rushed towards the phone to secure his peoples phone. The Homie didn't like how the Lion was coming towards him so when he got within range, he punched him in the face and scooped him up and smashed the Lion's head right on the blacktop. All of a sudden, the Lions rushed over as well as a few of the Bloods and the small group got to fighting and stabbing each other. The yard officers responded to the situation and handcuffed the men they caught and took them to the box. This was just the beginning of the shit storm that was about come.

I locked on the other side of the compound and we were locked in our cells that night. The way it worked was, one side went to that yard one night and other side would go the next night. During the day, I worked in the shipping part of the license plate shop. All day the Homies and the Lions were going at each other every time the cells opened. On my side of the jail there were at least 100 Bloods. There are sects under the Bloods, but with an outside enemy we all unite together. The administration knew what was going on and they heightened the security measures, but there was little they could do.

Auburn has 2 yards. A big center yard where the issues started the day before and small yard with weights. The Homies were on one side of the yard, and the Lions were at the top of the small yard. The tension was thick and my senses were on high alert. I didn't know exactly what was going to happen, but I had been through this enough to know something was about to go down.

The Jamaican population in A block was only about 25 dudes. It didn't even matter that some of them weren't Black Lions, because the situation had now turned into the Bloods against the Jamaicans. It was time to move so we broke up into smaller groups that would start moving to the top part of the yard. All of a sudden, they started rushing each other. It was like a scene straight out of Braveheart, a 100-guy free for all. You attacked whoever was in your way. The noise was so loud, and all you would hear were the sound of fists into flesh, or the screeches of grown men in pain after they were cut. It was just total chaos. Because of the heavy search there wasn't anything bigger than a razor being used. I was only fighting and I had a young Homie with me. I kept him close because he was nervous and with me, he would be safer than on his own.

The little homie and I had knocked our guy under the cement tables that were in the area when I heard the gun shot go off from the guard tower. The first shot was the warning shot but the next shot went into the crowd. The squad was on their way and I knew heads were about to get cracked in order for the CO's to gain control. We had to make it to the other side, but to do this, we would need to pass the officers shack. We had to get there before they locked the top half

205

down and tried to round up whoever they thought were involved. I grabbed the little homie who was still kicking the Jamaican we had under the table and we started fast walking right past the officers who were running to where we had just left. The little Homie and I weren't the only ones getting off the scene. A bunch of us made it to the other side of the yard before the officers trapped everyone else. Once we were safe on the other side, we watched as the cops escorted the few homies that were unable to get away. There wasn't one Jamaican left on A block after the riot.

There was another war going on over the phones in the yard. No one is ever happy because prison is full of miserable men. I wasn't the only one who had known loss. I was negotiating the terms of the phone when two guys came at me. The first had a razor and he tried to cut me in the face, but I slipped out of the way and punched the guy as hard as I could. The second kid was the cutters safety. (the safety is the back up to make sure the cutter doesn't get caught with the weapon) When the first guy missed and got punched in the face, the second guy started fighting with me. We fought until the cops broke it up, but I didn't get cut because the best defense is a strong offense sometimes. I'm too stupid to run and have too much pride to hide.

I was placed in keep-lock status for the assault awaiting the hearing which would decide how much time I would get. Keep-lock status is when an inmate is confined to his personal cell for 23 hours a day. I ended up refusing the hearing because I wasn't going to let them ask me any questions, because I wasn't giving them any answers. The inmates who were behind the attempt were now nervous because I was going to come off keep lock and I knew who was behind the attack. However, I wouldn't get the chance to ever see population in Auburn again.

While I was in Keep-lock status, a big situation happened between the officers and the Bloods. Things got out of control and the jail was locked down and this only made it worse. When the officers were coming into the cells to search, the fighting would start. The administration decided to transfer all high-ranking gang members on a Saturday. This doesn't happen on a weekend unless it's serious.

When the officers were coming to get us, we all had to be handcuffed before we were allowed to come out of the cells. Five officers escorted us. My cell was on the fifth floor and I thought they were going to try to throw me down the stairs, but they didn't. When I got downstairs I was placed facing the wall. I was handcuffed behind my back and to my surprise, my handcuffs were taken off and then I felt the punch to the back of my head. I have a built-in fight instinct in me. When I'm hit, I just go on autopilot. I am fortunate to have trained in hand to hand combat basically my entire life. I fought with the two officers who were sent to rough me up before I left their prison. I knew if I started doing any real damage, the other officers would have jumped in. I just fought enough to stay safe. They asked if I had enough, then re cuffed me and placed me into the holding cage until the bus came to get me and the other three homies that were leaving with me.

The four of us were loaded into a van at night and we left the facility. The officers who were taking us wouldn't tell us where we were going, so we guessed and joked around. The laughter would stop once we pulled up to Elmira Correctional Facility, a prison I lasted 12 days my first time there when I was 24 years old. When the van pulled up to the prison, the officer who circles the prison in a van asked our escorting officers, "Are these the assholes from Auburn?" The vans and buses go to the side of the prison to come in and drop the prisoners off. We pulled into the truck trap so they could check the arriving vehicles. The escorting officers told the truck trap officers, "They got tired of cutting each other and started cutting the staff". I knew at this point we were all about to get our asses kicked and I was right.

The van pulled into the prison and there was a squad of about 20 big officers waiting with their sticks out and ready for action. I knew what was about to happen because I had been through this before but one of the homies said, "What is that the intimidation squad?" These officers weren't there for show. Each prison has a group of cops they use when it was time to fuck dudes up, and this was Elmira's gang. I told the boys, "Get ready." No sooner than the words came out of my mouth, the side door slid open and we were being pulled out and cracked in the head with the sticks each officer held. There were three and four officers on each of us beating us with sticks. Each one of us had shackles on our legs and handcuffs that were locked to a chain around our waists. The officers beat on us for a steady five minutes that seemed like forever. I had been through this before, so I knew to lock my jaw, roll my shoulders and use my legs to kick them back. Chained up in the way we were didn't allow us to defend ourselves very well, but that was the point.

The officers pulled us back to our feet to take us to the hospital. On the walk to the prison infirmary the officers were taking random shots at us, but now they were just fists. When we got to the prison hospital the nurses were cursing at us and telling us to sign off on some papers. The Sergeant stated, "The white one is the big Homie." I was being called all sorts of nigger lover and other bullshit I have heard from racists my entire life. Now each one of us was placed in a hospital room by ourselves. I was still chained up and pretty bashed up but I was still alive, so it could have been worse. I hobbled over to where the mirror was and looked at the damage I could see. I went back to the bed and sat down, I knew they weren't finished with us yet.

After a couple of minutes two more officers came in. One was an older guy and the other a steroid outed young officer. I knew how this was going to play out. The Sergeant said, "Are you going to fight when I take the cuffs off?" Now mind you, I didn't have much fight left in me, but my pride wouldn't allow me to get beat like I had been and not do anything. The older officer undid my restraints and got out of the way. I jumped up with what little strength I had and made an effort to throw some punches before big boy was all over me. I was re-cuffed and pulled to my feet and back to the hallway.

I was the last one to come back out of the room. The cop said, "The white boy is the only one who fought back out of all you big bad gangsters". The officers laughed. We were now escorted to solitary confinement. The other guys who were with me were still getting punched but I was not. I can only guess as much that the officers may not have liked me, but they had to respect me because I wasn't a coward. By the time we were thrown into our cells, my whole body hurt. I called to the boys to make sure everyone was alive. In the box, some of the homies I had been in other prisons with were already down there. One of my good friends who was about to be sent to Massachusetts to start his 50-year sentence, was next to me and going to a visit the next day. I gave him my lawyers information and told him to have his girlfriend call and explain the situation. I couldn't eat the food because I didn't trust the officers weren't fucking with it.

Normally, when you arrive to a prison you're photographed immediately and given your ID. However, because we were beaten so severely, and the Department of Corrections was good at covering their tracks, we were not photographed or issued an ID until the evidence of their assault disappeared. After a couple of days, we were pulled out one at a time by a Security Captain. When this Captain pulled me out and said, "What happened to you?" I said, "I fell out of the van when we got here." This wasn't the first time I had gotten my ass kicked by CO's and sadly enough, it most likely won't be my last. If we made an issue over this, we would be charged with assault on a staff member and given a year or two in Solitary Confinement or a new charge. I knew how this worked and this was just part of life in prison.

I was taken out of the box and put on a tier that was for locked status inmates because I still had time from the Auburn assault. I was being pulled out of my cell and threatened by all sorts of security staff. I was being told if that shit from Auburn continued over here in Elmira, they would kill me. I didn't believe this, but I knew they would have no problem putting hands and feet on me. I didn't have anything to do with what happened in Auburn, but they believed I did.

When I finally got off Keep-lock status, the security had a meeting about me coming out. Everywhere I went, I was watched. Elmira has a recreation area they call the Fieldhouse. The Fieldhouse is basically a gym with an indoor running track, basketball courts, weights and showers. When I got into the Fieldhouse I was speaking to all the other little homies to see what was going on.

The officers who ran the Fieldhouse pulled me into their office. The officer who pulled me in said, "We're just wondering why everyone wants to talk to you?" I may not be that smart, but I think fast on my feet. I said, "I have been in prison a long time and I know a lot of people". He said, "Dutch, that was a good answer, but we know who you are. There was a security meeting this morning stating you would be released in general population." I said, "I don't want any problems." The Sergeant looked at me and said, "You were here in 1999, you cut the Latin King in this very Fieldhouse and then chased him across the basketball court until an officer close lined you." This was exactly what happened. I was dumbfounded because I hardly remembered that because I was a young stupid kid back then. The Sergeant said, "I was your company officer back then before I became a Sergeant." I said, "I am not the same man I was back then. I am trying to change my life and get back to Eastern to finish my college degree. All I want to do is paint and get out of prison."

I'm sure the staff was skeptical because it was easier to believe I was still the old me. The problem was, I was still dealing with my Gang members who were up to the same old nonsense. I had lost the love of my life because of my gang involvement and because I couldn't keep my ass out of trouble. I was really trying to change. The Sergeant called the officers in my housing unit and they told me to bring pictures of my work to the Fieldhouse. I grabbed a few of my paintings and went out. I showed my work and the staff was impressed. I was asked to do a couple of murals in the Fieldhouse. I agreed and got to work. I did a 20-foot Buffalo Bills Logo the Warden wanted, a huge seascape and I also touched up the work of another artist who was before me. I was trying to stay out of trouble, but to make a real change, I would be tested by a power greater than me.

I wanted everything, but the question was, what would I be willing to give up in order to get what I wanted and needed? I have been blessed with many gifts I used for the wrong causes and I was only starting to understand the concept of planting good seeds to get good harvests. The same shit I had done in the streets was more or less the same shit I was doing in prison. I didn't like the way I was living my life. I was about to be tested and my choice would lead me down a path that was unfamiliar, but the reward would be what I had really wanted. Love, hope and perhaps a normal life.

* * * * * *

I was told another inmate needed to be dealt with because of a gang matter and I was the only one with the skills to handle this guy. I knew the man when he was a big Homie of the Bloods. I also knew the real reason the President of the council wanted this guy (who happened to be his cousin) dealt with. The issue was over a girl and drugs, yet the president was using propaganda to handle his personal vendettas. This is not supposed to be allowed because we were supposed to be the vanguard of the oppressed.

When I got to the top, I saw the truth of things and didn't like what I saw. The cause I once believed in, wasn't real. It's a devastating reality when you realize what you believed in was fake. I truly believed we were going to make a change, that we were going to create something that meant something. A few bad apples made our cause look bad and I believed I had sacrificed so much already. I didn't want to continue to sacrifice for something I didn't believe in anymore. I felt like I was being used when I was being asked to do something to a man who didn't deserve it. I wanted more out of life. I just needed something more.

My 39th Birthday was about to be upon me when I had to make this choice. My sister and her daughter were flying up to see me, and I had to make sure I didn't lose my visits prior to this. My sister showed up with my niece. I couldn't believe it, she wasn't a baby anymore and she

211

was so smart. My niece looked at me and said, "How do people transport drugs from country to country." I was shocked. She was only 14 years old and this made me worry. When she got up to use the bathroom, I looked at my sister and said, "What the fuck?" My sister said, "She is not using drugs, I had her tested. I have no idea where she came up with this, but she was researching on the internet." I said, "How do you want me to respond to this?" Heather said, "You may as well answer her questions because she is going to find out one way or another." My niece sat back down at the table, and we resumed our talk. In my opinion, she had entirely too much information and I couldn't believe she was able to find out this type of the stuff on the internet. At this point in my life, I had been in prison for 17 years and I had never been on the internet.

After we ate lunch, I started to explain to Heather how I felt and what I had been going through. I said, "I may have to end up taking care of some gang business, and I am not sure what the outcome will be." My sister looked me dead in the eyes and said, "Do you like prison?" With a snotty tone, I said, "Of course I don't fucking like prison!" Heather said, "It is difficult to tell because you keep making choices that aren't helping you come home." I just looked at her and she said, "You continue to be loyal to people who don't give a fuck about you." I knew she was right. As I sat there I was thinking about how I lost the love of my life due to my poor decisions and loyalty to my gang members. At this very moment, I decided I was going to try a different path.

It was easy for me to do wrong because I had been doing wrong my entire life. I could have sumped that guy, gone to the box and the Homies would have loved me. I would have been the good soldier I had always been, but I just couldn't do it anymore. I knew taking a stance would cause me problems, yet my choice would be on the side of the right. I refused the order and expressed that the hit was not what it was being portrayed to be. My stance would threaten the influence of power and I knew this would come with repercussions. I told all the other Gang members I was no longer Blood. It was not this easy for a man of my rank to walk away, but I was done. I felt I deserved more out of life because I now believed I could be more than I was. I would rather be known as an artist than a gangster.

I knew they were going to send someone at me, because they needed to show that there were consequences to disobeying orders. I am a good fighter and I knew who ever came for me would be armed with weapons, but I wouldn't start and I would not use a weapon. I was only going to defend myself. This wasn't the smartest move, but I had set my mind to change and whatever was going to happen was going to happen.

I was outside on a hot August night and another block of inmates was mixing with my blocks recreation time due to a softball game. I knew what was going on when I saw ¾ of the team were Bloods. I went over to the dugout and addressed the situation to the Homies. I said, "A call has been made for the assault of another homie that was not just, but based on personal beef. It doesn't matter where the order came from, because right is right and wrong is wrong and every one of us has rules to live by." One of the little Homies said, "Listen big bro, the call was made." I said, "I do not take orders from little Homies and if you feel some sort of way, do what you gotta do." At this point, no one directly wanted to step up to me, but I knew they would start plotting.

Attacks are usually on the sneak, but it's difficult to sneak a dude who knows the routine. I walked over to the phone and called one of my friends. I told him I was about to get into some nonsense. As I was on the phone, I was watching the guys put together their attack squad. I saw the 3 guys when they came up, and when they got close enough I saw the weapon in the lead guys hand. I dropped the phone and got to fighting before he could swing the razor. My attackers were on me, but they didn't get to cut me. I fought all of them until the police broke up the fight. I was fine, but the kid with the razor ended up with a broken jaw.

I was handcuffed and escorted out of the yard and placed against the wall in the Fieldhouse. I looked over to the Sergeant and said, "God damn, I am getting old." He said, "It's hard to tell because that kids jaw is sitting on his chest." I said, "When I was younger, they all would have ended up this way." The Sergeant laughed because he thought this was funny. The officers enjoyed the drama that comes with the day to day life of prison as long as it doesn't involve their staff.

I was placed on keep lock status for 30 days. While I was locked up, I sent word how I just wanted to be left alone and how I wouldn't transgress, but I would defend myself. I knew they wouldn't leave me alone, but I wasn't going to allow my life to be in someone else's hands anymore. As a gang member, you must take on the problems of your brothers and I was washing my hands of this. I was done.

I had men from different gangs and prison organizations who wanted to step in and help me, but I had gotten myself into all this bullshit and I didn't want anyone to get caught up in my mess. This was a road I would have to travel alone. The officers who once hated me now respected me because I was standing up for myself against serious odds. The administration knew what was going on, but I refused to tell because I was getting what I deserved for the things I did. I just put my trust in God and I hoped he would lead me down the road he wanted me to be on.

I had three gang related fights before the administration stepped in and placed me in segregation. In segregation, I was placed on a tier with very few people and we were kept away from the general population. I could paint and work, but I was lonely. Joy had been gone for almost ten years now. Other women would reach out to me but they weren't her. For almost ten years I prayed every night for her to return to me. My faith was constantly tested because nothing seemed to be getting better for me. I had created a board game, an adult coloring book, and painted a bunch of paintings but couldn't make my art turn a profit due to being in prison. I was getting very frustrated.

Prison is a very dangerous place for a man who is battling with the demons of depression. I started to question everything. Why couldn't anyone love me, was I just no better than a criminal, would anyone care if I was dead and a bunch of other deep dark thoughts. These were difficult realities to me, because I always felt like I was the man. In reality, I was no more or no less than the men in the cells next to me. I started to have visions of cutting my wrists or forcing the guard tower to shoot me. The only peace I would find would be under the influence of drugs.

I wrote my mother explaining how I had reoccurring visions of my death and told her what my wishes were for after my death. I wanted to make sure she buried me in my own clothes, and I told her exactly what I wanted to wear. My mother's responses were filled with worry, yet she didn't know what to tell me. She attempted to provide me with reasons as to why I should continue living my life. She told me there were people who cared about me and when I came home, I would be ok. But most of all, she told me how it would devastate her. When I was young, I believed taking your own life was a sign of weakness but as I contemplated taking my own life, I realized it took a certain type of strength and dedication.

I felt as though I needed to leave something behind. I didn't want to only be remembered for my life of crime so I decided to write my life story. My life was far from normal, but I felt I had a story to tell. With my story being told, I also believed the artwork I left behind would have more meaning. I had a few extra black and white marbled notebooks from when I attended college, so I started to write. I wrote hours a day, for months. I didn't know if my mother would ever do anything with the book, but I still wanted to have my story on paper.

There were two women I hoped my death would punish for the hurt they inflicted upon me. One was the only woman I had ever loved in my life, and the other was the woman who was supposed to love me since the day I was born. I knew how important closure was, and with death, certain questions would never be answered. I needed these

215

people to question if they were ever important to me, because they forced me to question if I was ever important to them.

FIFTEEN

PAST, PRESENT & FUTURE

"You're my drug, breathe you in till my face numb"
-Machine Gun Kelly

From "Handguns to Paintbrushes" started out as my last-ditch effort to leave my story behind. I had just had enough. Sometimes a man needs to hit rock bottom and my life was filled with highs and lows, but the difference now was, I now knew I was my own worst enemy. It's a hard truth to swallow how everything in your life is your fault. It's always easier when you can blame someone else.

I was at my breaking point when one day the CO came to my cell and dropped an envelope with a handwriting I knew, even though it had been years since I'd seen it.

Jeff,

It's been over 9 years since we have spoken. I have no excuses for how I went about things, but life just happened. I guess I just wasn't strong enough to do it. I just couldn't do it. I have thought

217

about you daily for over 9 years. This is a letter I have been trying to write for 9 years. Of course, I found someone, I moved on. . .Life happened and I was lonely. I don't have a real reason, just excuses. I guess I just wasn't strong enough to do this, and just didn't know how to tell you. I just couldn't love you from afar anymore. Don't worry, I received my share of Karma. You have no idea what I have been through, and I will spare telling you the details unless you ask. . .

I just wanted to say I am sorry. You've been the love of my life since high school, but I was so broken. You just don't know. You will never know how loving you affected me. . .You saved me at a time where I thought I couldn't be saved.

My father died unexpectedly and this has truly broken me. I don't think I will ever be the same. I don't want to write too much or go into too much detail, because after all, I don't know if you even want to hear from me. I just left you for dead, and there is nothing else I can do but say I'm sorry. I truly am Jeff. I never meant to hurt you. I know you don't believe this, but. . . it is the truth. If I don't hear from you I completely understand, but if you have any questions at all, I am ready to answer them.

Joy

I couldn't believe it was her. It wasn't what I wanted to hear, but it was a start. My thoughts were all over the place. She had broken my heart when she left me, but her leaving caused me to look deep within and make changes that were needed. My feelings were a whirlwind. I wanted to be mad and I was, but I also had hope that I would be able to have the only woman who ever mattered to me. I wrote her back immediately.

Joy,

You have caught me at a loss for words and this is rare. I don't know how I feel because you fucked me up. You're the only woman I have loved in my life. You don't need to tell me how long it has been, because I've thought about you every day. It's nice to hear you moved on, because I never did. You're right, you don't have a good reason for what you did because I was head over heels in love with you and you were getting on with your life. You left me for dead like everyone else in my life. I can understand how you wanted a man who was home, but I have always had to ask myself what's wrong with me that I'm the only person who cares about Jeff. It's easier to think of me the way you remember someone who has passed away. You claimed I saved you at a time where you thought you couldn't be saved. It's funny the way you repaid me.

I'm sorry to hear about your father. I lost grandma and you know how I felt about her. My life is fucked up because after you abandoned me, I went crazy and I really hoped I would get killed behind these walls. I don't know if this letter makes any kind of sense, because on one hand I love you more than you will ever know, but on the other hand I want to spit in your face because you were supposed to love me for the rest of my life. I don't know what I am supposed to say to you, you didn't even care about me enough to pay me the respect of coming to tell me face to face. I understand more than you think because I understand this life of mine is fucked up. I want to hear from you, I would never shut you out because I'm not you, but you are not forgiven. I don't know what you want from me. I have shit going on because I'm trying to set up my life because once I get out of prison, I'm not coming back. I am writing a book, "from handguns to paint brushes; how art changed my life". I am really good at painting and drawing now. I was in two different college programs, but I keep getting kicked out of these prisons. Right now I am in ad-seg because I told them I was done and they sent the hit squad at me 3 different times and couldn't get the job done. I ended up hurting them each time. I am not about to have shit go down like when I was hit in Greenhaven. I'm just tired of all this shit, I want to go home. I have now spent more time in prison than I have free. I almost married a girl I hated just because I was tired of being alone.

As I am sitting here writing this, I cannot figure out how I feel about you because I will always be in love with you. I didn't know I was capable of loving anyone until I was with you, but you hurt me really bad. I'm not the same man I was and it's because when you left I shut off my feelings. I want to know love and be happy, but I have not been happy for a long time. Now you write me this short bull-shit letter? You didn't care about me then so why now? In your letter you told me, "of course I found someone, I moved on". Is this statement supposed to make me feel better? The thought of you with another man makes me want to kill someone.

I would like to think we could be friends but I don't know. If you would've told me you weren't strong enough to do this and you deserve better than me, I would understand all this. Why didn't you put a cell phone # or something? I think I want to talk to you, but I really want to look into your eyes, but this isn't going to happen. This letter is written as if I have no education but you have my mind all over the place. I'm not going to write anymore, but your response better have more substance than this sorry ass letter you didn't even spend enough time to hand write. I'm going to put some questions on the back. You say you're ready to give me answers.

-The guy you found, was it worth it?

-Are you married/with someone now?

-Why didn't you give me the face to face you promised me?

-Do you still love me?

-What do you want from me?

-Why should I accept your apology?

-Why would I trust you?

-When you close your eyes, can you still see my face?

-Do you miss me?

-How are the kids?

-Why did it take almost 10 years to get this letter?

Dutch

I couldn't sleep and I couldn't stop thinking about her. I was frustrated when I wrote the first letter, but I spent the night reflecting on how much she meant to me. I had grown so much and I wanted to show her how I changed. I wanted another shot but this woman had left me for dead. Could I forgive her? My first letter to her was filled with raw emotion and wasn't exactly nice, but I said things I needed to say. The next day I decided to write her again.

Dear Joy

Yesterday's letter was not well planned out because I was conflicted over how I felt. You have to understand that you were the only good thing in my life because our love was pure in a world that is evil. You claim my love for you saved you, yet look at the flip side. I am a man who has lived a life of deceit, violence and other evils all in the pursuit of money and power. This is not who I am at the core of my being, however, I was able to thrive. Once you were gone I was bangin all day.

221

You have to understand that you are the only woman in my life I felt loved me for me, not who I was in the streets or because of my family. With you I realized what it was to love someone for everything they are, as well as everything they are not. No one is without flaws and if you know the worst thing about a person and can look passed it because you love them, this is something you cherish.

I have been abandoned by everyone who was supposed to love me. You knew I had trust issues because of what I endured as a child. It hurt me when you abandoned me because I had finally felt like someone truly loved me. It hurt me because I knew you would move on and even though I tried, I couldn't. I have spent years of this time alone because none of them were you. When I almost married Rachael she used to come on the visits and ask why I wasn't all over her, etc. I have never been a man who is willing to settle for less than I feel I deserve. Do you know what I was going through with the thought of marrying a woman I couldn't stand?

When your letter came and just with a quick glance at the envelope, I knew it was you. I really don't know what you want from me, but please don't hurt me again, you're the only person in the world who has the ability to do so. I still love you, even though I am not sure I like you.

I started painting 6 years ago because I needed a way to escape. I found myself getting better really fast so I took my time and learned as much as I could. The more I painted, the more I started to change, plus this was the time I first got into college. The problem was, I was trying to do it all. I didn't want to do all this time and not make a way for myself. I have donated pieces I've done to different things and I started writing my book, a story about my life. I have amassed a large body of work. In the art world, the artist's story is as important as the work and o boy, do I have a story to tell.

I just have to stop putting my hands on these dudes, but when I try to be easy, they try their hands. Albany has run out of places to send me. This isn't who I am anymore. I have to be able to look into the mirror and be proud of who I see. The street life doesn't have a happy ending in real life. I have become bitter because my life was supposed to be so much more than prison. I am the one who fucked up my life and this is a hard reality to accept. You know who are strong and deserve respect? Men who bust their asses every day to take care of their families. People fear men like me, but fear is only for a minute and love is forever.

I hope this letter is more coherent than the one from yesterday. I want to hear from you, but remember, we don't lie to each other and I won't ask anything I cannot deal with the answer to. I will be waiting. . .

Jeff

I was still so in love with her, and waiting day after day to receive her response was killing me. I started to get nervous and thought maybe she wasn't going to write back. Last time I left so many of my true feelings unsaid. I still had so much to say to her so I decided to write her one more letter.

Dear Joy,

I have been counting down the days till I get a response from my letters to you. I have waited over 9 years to hear from you and now the week I have to wait for a response is far too long. I have a weak spot for you, I should hate you, yet it isn't possible.

The difference between you and me is, I knew I couldn't be happy with anyone else and you tried to replace me. How did this workout for you? Do you not understand that we are supposed to be together? It just hurts that you don't care about me enough to believe in me or us. This was the hardest part of the whole thing.

I want to talk to you. I am going to send you money to put on the phone. I need to hear your voice for a few hours. I have missed you. I will not ask you anything I don't want to know the answer to. You know how I am. Life is crazy and I understand more than you may think I do.

My last girlfriend was a young Spanish girl. She was cool but she wasn't you and no other woman who may come into my life will ever be you. You will always be my princess, even if you never become my wife. I knew love when you were in my life and this was the only time. I've known lust but only love and lust with you.

When I lost you I had a lot of time to learn about myself as well as what I wanted out of life. I am not the same man, but in some ways, I am still the same 15-year-old boy you fell in love with two life time's ago. I'm not as handsome as I used to be back then, but what I lost in looks I've made up for in wit.

I know you deserve better than me, but I know there isn't another man in the whole world who can love you the way I do. Our problem is, I don't know if I could ever be your friend because I don't believe that I could be in a room with you and not hold you in my arms. I want to kill any man who touches you or ever has so I don't know if we could just be friends. I don't know, maybe you don't love me anymore.

You don't miss me? You don't want to look at me with those big beautiful brown eyes? You don't miss looking into the eyes of a man who loves you more than anything in life? You said you would answer my questions. I used to believe money and power were the most important things in life and I've had both and I wasn't happy. Do you know when I was happy? I was happy when I would walk into a prison visiting room and lock eyes with you and I would pull you close to me and hold you while I kissed you. This was when I was happy.

I can close my eyes and see your face as a little girl and as a grown woman. I don't even know what some of the faces of women I had sex with look like, but you, you're my happy place. I'm a fucked-up guy and maybe I don't deserve to be happy due to all the foul shit I have done in life. But I will only be happy with you. Please don't make me be with another woman. Why can't I be with the woman I love? I know I'm supposed to be all cool and act like everything's your fault, but I know I was fucking up and getting bounced all over the place and at the time, I still had so long to go. I learned to love and appreciate you more when I didn't have you because I loved you so much and I couldn't have you.

I was miserable without you and banged real hard because I hated everyone. You are the only goodness in my life and without you I was cold. You can never understand parts of me because you didn't grow up the way I did. I have trust issues because everyone has abandoned me. My family is cold. My mom and I now have a better relationship, but the woman who pushed me out still doesn't want anything to do with me. I was this woman's first child. I have had to work on my issues because my issues are the ones that fed the monster who lays within me. By nature, I am very loyal, but I feel I never get loyalty in return.

When I got into college and started reading all these different books and getting good grades I started to believe I could be more. I want to live life, but without you, my life will never be complete. I used to find you very attractive, but I'm in love with you on so much more of a deeper level and this is what you don't get. To hold you in my arms is to embrace true love.

Your pictures are still in my photo albums. Everyone who knows me knows about you, because even when you were gone, I held onto you. You didn't want me, but I have always wanted you. I have needed to tell you these things for all these years. Your letter sounded like you were worried if I wanted to speak to you or not. I wish I could talk to you for the rest of my life. I don't know what is going to transpire between us, but I want you to know that I will love you for the rest of my life. I hope you sent a phone # so I can speak to you.

Jeff

Ten days after I received her first letter, I finally received the answer to her questions with her phone number.

The guy you found, was it worth it? No.

Are you married/with someone now? No.

Why didn't you give me the face to face you promised me? I couldn't tell you I was leaving because you would have said, "You don't love me anymore?" and I did. I have always loved you Jeff, I just couldn't deal with your life in prison anymore. And would you have just let me leave? Answer this honestly? Would you have just understood? No.

226

Do you still love me? I always have and I always will.

What do you want from me? I wanted to make sure you were ok and I don't know.

Why should I accept your apology? You shouldn't.

Why would I trust you? I don't know.

When you close your eyes, can you still see my face? I do. I have thought about you every day for almost 10 years.

Do you miss me? I do.

How are the kids? They're well.

Why did it take almost ten years to get this letter? I've been trying to write you for years but I just didn't know what to say.

She detailed some of what had been going on in her life for the past 10 years in her letter. She was with some loser who constantly cheated on her. This was very difficult for me to hear and even more difficult for me to accept. I immediately contacted her via 3-way and heard a voice I hadn't heard in almost 10 years. As much as I wanted to be angry with her, I just couldn't. I had missed this girl every day she was gone and I was still so head over heels in love with her. We spoke about her life and I was very cautious with the questions I asked her. I expected her to be honest and truthful with me, but I also told her I would not ask anything I couldn't deal with the answer to.

I had asked her how her kids were in my first letter, and she responded with, "They are well". We were speaking on the phone when suddenly, she blurted out, "I had a baby, well not so much a baby anymore but I had a little boy who just turned 9 a few days ago." I couldn't believe what I was hearing. I was shocked and this killed me. I went off, "You had a baby? And he just turned nine years old? This means you were pregnant the last time I spoke with you? I asked you if you were with anyone else and you told me you weren't. You fucking lied to me, a baby, you had a fucking baby with this loser?" She said, "Yes, I did and I love this little boy more than life itself." I was in shock and I eventually responded with, "Of course you do because you're an amazing mother, you have always been an amazing mom." It was a lot for me to digest. Not only did she leave me for dead for some loser who cheated on her, she had a baby with this idiot after telling me she never wanted to have any more kids. Hearing this had me beyond fucked up.

The guy she cheated on me with was the dude she told me she went out on a date with during our last visit. Not only did she cheat, she lied to me and left me for dead in prison after promising to love me forever. She had a life and a child with this loser. My emotions were all over the place. The truth doesn't always set you free. This truth broke me down. Here was the only woman I had ever loved and she destroyed me. As a gang leader, I only made choices against my soldiers if their actions were malicious.

I was beyond confused. I loved this woman but I had just spent 10 years of my life, wondering if what we had was even real. I didn't know the truth as to what happened and I drove myself insane for years, but I loved her. My love for her never stopped. I had taken this girl for granted because I knew I loved her, but I was also living my life in prison ten years earlier like I had no intentions of coming home. I had asked her to do something I should have never asked of her. I was finally at the point in my life where I had to truly own up to my own actions. Had I pushed the love of my life into the arms of another dude? When I asked myself this question and the truth looked me in the face, I wanted to smash the mirror.

* * * * * *

Joy had two children when she came back into my life the first time when I was in Greenhaven, yet when we used to talk about our future, Joy told me she didn't want to have any more kids. And here she was with a child she decided to have with a dude that I didn't consider to be even close to my level. The daughter I thought was mine wasn't mine and now the woman who I loved and always wanted to have a child with, had a child with the man she cheated on me with. It was a lot to handle and I felt like God was trying to beat me up even more at this point. My pride was hurt and I wondered how could I accept all of this? I was Jeff D, or at least I was, but what was I now?

I was a man who had hurt people for financial gain. I was a man who had to use drugs to deal with the reality of my fucked-up life. I was a man who a month before Joy coming back into my life, was writing this very book so I could have my story told because I had planned on taking my own life. I was a man who had contracts on my head by the very gang I was once a leader of, the gang I chose over everything else, the gang I finally walked away from. I was a man who wasn't happy.

While I was trying to work through all the madness, the love of my life was telling me she just wanted to be my friend and make sure I was alright. In the beginning, Joy and I just talked on the phone. I guess you can say we were trying to slip back into our comfort zone. I was still so in love with this girl. I would always ask her, "Can I have hope?" and she would say, "No, I just want to be your friend." The thing is, we both knew we couldn't just be friends, our feelings have always been too deep to just be friends. It was all or nothing with us, and I wanted the love of my life back. Even if she didn't want to admit it at first, I knew she still loved me and I was still so in love with her.

Our "friendship" only lasted a few weeks. I remained insecure and I was afraid I was going to lose her again, but I promised myself if she chose to leave again, I wouldn't allow her to leave without knowing exactly how much she meant to me. The years I spent without Joy had taught me how I needed to love her because the unanswered questions of why she left, caused me to break down and analyze every aspect of our relationship.

We spoke daily. My phone calls to Joy were so important to me because I just needed to hear her voice, but at times, it was very difficult for me. I tried to understand how she had a lot of guilt because of what she put me through and how she just wanted to be honest with me. But I knew how I was and I also knew what I could deal with. I told Joy I would never ask her anything I wouldn't be able to deal with the answer to.

I received a letter one day from her detailing her relationship with the man she cheated, left me for and had a baby with. It was too much for me to handle and I lost it. This is the woman who promised to love me forever, this was the woman who has loved me since she was a little girl, this was the woman I was head over heels in love with, but this was also the woman who destroyed me. Was I fucked up and troubled? Yes. But I always made her feel loved and she just left me, without a word for 10 fucking years.

I called her the afternoon after I received her letter and I tried to keep myself calm but I was unable to. As soon as she said, "Hi" I went off and said, "I want you to listen to me very carefully and do not say a word." She said, "Ok" and I said, "How could you possibly say the things you said to me in that letter? I now have visions of him sleeping with you, like I can physically see him touching you Joy and this makes me fucking crazy." I was so in love with this girl, but I was petrified to lose her. She had this power over me and it drove me crazy. I yelled, "I fucking love you Joy, but I am afraid to lose you because I have before." She was silent and I just started to break down and cry. She just said, "I am so sorry for all I put you through. I don't know what else I can say." She was right, there was nothing else she could say that would change what she had done. It was time to get off the phone and we said goodbye. I was fucked up after this phone call. I went back to my cell

230

and wrote to her. I was pissed off at all she put me through, but the truth was, I loved her and I needed her.

Joy

> *You say it is over but he is there and I'm not and if I was home, I know what I would do to get you back. I worry about when he realizes you are the one and only. I wouldn't be able to be free and not do everything in my power to get you back. You say he doesn't love you like I do, but I cannot see how any man who knows you couldn't love you as I do. I worry about losing you because I have before.*
>
> *I need you to promise you'll never leave me again. You will never have to worry about me cheating on you or even question if I love you because you are my one and only princess. We are going to argue just because that's how we always do, but I will never let you go to sleep mad at me if I can control it. I love you momma and I can't imagine my life without you in it. I know if I love you as much as I say I do I should want you to be happy even if it isn't with me, but I can't. I'm sorry, I can't."*

Jeff

* * * * * *

Joy and I had only been speaking for a few months, but with us it felt like we had never stopped speaking. I hadn't been happy in a very long time but she made me happy again. As we were talking one day she said to me, "I want to marry you Jeff and I don't care if we have to get married in prison." I immediately said, "No. You don't want to marry me in prison. You didn't want to back then and I know you don't want to now. You always wanted our beach wedding even if it was just the two of us on the beach. Now that I have you back, I will never pressure you to do anything I know you don't want to do ever again."

New York is one of the only states left that offers conjugal visits. If we were married, we would be able to spend an entire weekend together alone every 3 months in an apartment located in the prison. I wanted to marry Joy back then and I guess you can say I kind of pressured her to get married, but a prison wedding was beneath her. She always shot me down with, "I am not going to marry the love of my life in prison." The weddings are performed in the visiting room during visiting times. The ceremonies aren't exactly special, they don't even last five minutes. We have seen other couples get married before and she would just look at me and say, "Eh no." This never deterred me from asking though. Of course, I wanted to marry her because she was the love of my life, but we would also be able to be alone for 48 hours and have a lot of sex. So yes, I really wanted to get married.

We went back and forth for days about getting married, I stuck to my guns and told her there was nothing she could do to convince me otherwise. I said, "My mind is made up and I am sorry but we are not getting married in prison." Joy said, "If you love me you will marry me, but if you're not sure if you love me, I understand why you can't marry me." I couldn't believe she was trying to manipulate me by saying I wouldn't marry her because I was not sure if I loved her. As usual, she got her way.

The next morning, I called Joy and said, "Can you manage to be quiet for a few minutes, is this possible? I know this is not the way it was supposed to be, and this is not the way we both would like to do this but. . .I have loved you since you were a little girl, but I truly fell in love with you as a grown woman. Our love is special and one of a kind. We have both made mistakes along our travels, yet, our love not only endured but became stronger. If you will have me, I'd like to spend the rest of my life trying to make you happy. You have always been my princess, but I am asking you to become my wife. Will you become Mrs. de Leyer and promise to love me for the rest of your life? That is, if you're not doing anything more important." She started to cry and said, "Yes, of course I will marry you."

232

I hadn't seen Joy in 10 years, but I was so in love with this girl, I asked her to marry me before she even visited. The truth of what happened was harder to deal with than anything I had ever dealt with. It was hard when she left because I didn't know why she left or even that she was leaving. For years, I tortured myself because I was trying to find the answers she never gave me. Now I knew the truth of the past 10 years and the truth bothered me. She left me and decided to build a life with some dude who treated her like shit. I couldn't understand how she stayed with a man who constantly cheated on her. This dude had the best woman, my woman and he treated her like crap but he was the one who got the best years of her life and a son. This was a lot to take in, and it was a lot for me to deal with.

We were on the phone one afternoon and she said, "Guess who is coming to see you tomorrow?" I couldn't believe she was coming. My emotions were all over the place. I knew this visit would either wash away the past or kill our future. I knew I loved her, but would love really be enough this time? I needed to see her to know if my memories of how she used to make me feel were real, or what I wanted to remember.

I hardly slept the night before. All I could do was think of her and everything we had been through since we were kids. In the morning, I was trying to get ready and focus my mind. Joy kept telling me she got old and fat, but with her, it has always been hard to tell what is fact and what is her imagination. She has always had a distorted body image and she battled with an eating disorder for many years. I loved this girl and I needed her to feel beautiful no matter what the situation was so I tried to prepare myself for anything. This was a lot of pressure because I loved this woman and I did not want to cause her any pain.

The visits start at 9am and when I last talked to her the night before, she was driving to NY. She was staying at a hotel close to the prison, but when I woke up there was snow on the ground and it was coming down hard. I was showered and ready, but I felt like time was at a standstill. When 10am rolled around, I started to get nervous and wondered if she was catching cold feet. I heard the officer's jingling keys downstairs and I was about to beg him for an emergency call when he called up to me and said, "de Leyer on the visit." My nerves began to wash away as I walked to the visiting room.

As soon as I walked in I saw her. Yes, she had put on some weight but she was still so breathtaking. I checked in with the officer and made my way to the table. I just looked at her and there she was, looking up at me with those big brown eyes and the same cute little smile. I grabbed her hands and pulled her into my arms and we kissed. When I kissed her it felt like it always had. I can't explain it, like a warm feeling and flashes throughout my body or something like that. I had never felt this way with any other woman before, but with her it has always been different. She always made me feel funny and warm.

When I sat down, I just couldn't take my eyes off her. She was absolutely beautiful. I was in prison which is not exactly the most romantic place to be with the woman you love, but I had always tried to make the best of my situation. She was just looking at me and smiling and I said, "Pretty girl, close your eyes and give me your hands." I had a little piece of pink yarn I wrapped around the button of my pants. Inmates are searched before and after a visit and I didn't know if they would allow it to go through. I removed the pink yarn and tied it around her ring finger on her left hand. When she opened her eyes, she looked down at her hands and smiled and said, " I love you." Today, she still has the little piece of yarn tied around her finger. She calls it her "pink string ring" She tells me she doesn't want to wear a wedding ring or engagement ring, she only wants her "pink string ring."

I grew up Catholic and was forced to go to church but I still always believe in a power greater than myself. I prayed every night with the mindset that it couldn't hurt, and if there was any truth to the teaching, that at least I had some degree of faith to set forth on judgement day. I prayed every night for God to send her back to me. I would pray for my family, friends, sick kids, anything to be honest. But these prayers were more about feeling like all my prayers shouldn't be selfish and just maybe if I put some unselfish requests in, it would help my cause. I have always been a wheeler and dealer and even in prayer, I was trying to make the deal.

In prison, inmates can attend different religious services and I popped up at different ones to see if the answers I needed could be found. One preacher told me something that made sense. He said, "God answers all prayers, the thing is, sometimes the answer is a no or a not right now." My prayers were finally answered and I realize that for many years the answer was, "not right now". I truly believe I wasn't ready to have Joy back in my life then because I would have never been able to deal with what had happened in her life. Back then, my pride still affected my decision making and I had a habit of passing judgement on people as if I had the right.

I love Joy and when she came back into my life, I was finally at a point where I could think about other people's needs. I finally realized that love was more powerful than fear. I was ready to be happy and I believed I finally had the ability to make someone else happy. I felt good for the first time in a very long time. I needed her, and as it turned out, she needed me too. I am working daily to accept what has happened in her life. I am not going to lie, it is difficult at times, but I love her and I know she is worth it. Sometimes things don't always work out as intended, but if it is meant to be, it is just meant to be. We are made for each other, I truly believe this. We have something I am not too sure many people have experienced.

As a young man, I was all about Jeff because I didn't want to let anyone in. When Joy was with me, she opened a door no one else could open. I spent years chasing the feelings only she could give me. I love her, I love being in love with her and I just can't live without her.

SIXTEEN

THE BEGINNING

"You've got a new story to write and it looks nothing like your past." -Danielle LaPorte

Change is difficult for many men and it is a day to day struggle for me. I have spent so much of my life on drugs and living a life of crime, this lifestyle had become the norm for me. It was very difficult for me to leave the gang life alone, because in the administration and most prisoner's eyes, I will always be Dutch Blood. However, Dutch is now an artist. For a man to really make a change it is easiest done by changing the people, places and things in one's life. The fact of the matter is, I am still in prison with the same people and same things that test me daily, but I have traveled too far head, to allow myself to backslide.

There are times I see men who I have genuine affection for, due to things we have been through together, but only say hello and keep it moving. I have spent too many years of my life trying to appease and impress people who didn't care about me. I now live for the people who really matter to me and the ones who have my best interests at heart. I have caused pain to many people and I must live with this.

My mentality was that of a boy, well into my 30's. I wanted to be young forever, but I no longer want this. I just want to have a normal life. In prison, a man has a lot of time to think about the things he misses. In my youth, I would have told whoever asked me I missed three things; Money, Power and Pussy. This would be the answer of many prisoner's right now. But today, I feel differently. Today I know money doesn't make you happy. I also know power is perceived in the streets due to fear. Once upon a time I would rather be feared than loved, but now I would rather be loved than feared because love has the ability to create all that is good. Last but not least is sex. Of course, I miss this, however, sex with someone you don't love is just that. I am now in love and I want to experience making love. Something I have never known before I fell head over heels in love with Joy.

I still have a lot of growing up to do and my art and Joy keep me focused. The sad truth is, a couple of years ago I wouldn't have been ready to become a productive member of society. I had to accept that I was my own worst enemy before I could make a change. Accepting this was a very difficult pill to swallow. I have to believe I am alive for a reason when so many others are not. Did prison save my life? This is scary because I have been through so much in here. I have been stabbed, cut, beat by the officers, etc. But the truth is, prison did save my life.

I am now looking forward to what my future may hold because I now have faith and hope, something I've never had before. I have faith the people in my corner are going to be there for me once I am released because they love me. I have hope that I will be able to make my dreams come true because of my good work ethic and perseverance.

One day I was deep in thought about my life and a question came to me; "What will you be remembered for?" I do not want the sum of my life to be my rap sheet and life of crime. I would much rather my young life of bad decision making be the path that led me on to whatever I will become as the new me. I would love to come home and do gallery shows where I can showcase my work and tell my story, but if this doesn't happen, I will find my niche in the world. I will continue to paint and draw until the day I die. I spent so many years destroying everything I touched, it is amazing to finally be able to create.

Throughout my life there have been many forks in the road and if I would have chosen a different path, my life may have turned out differently. The problem was, I was young and stupid and didn't understand the consequences of my actions. The only woman I ever loved, the woman who has loved me since she was a little girl couldn't stay with me due to my choices and actions. It took me to lose the love of my life to realize I needed to change. She loved me unconditionally, but she could only put up with so much. I sat locked in a cage with nothing but my thoughts. I spent years of my life angry until one day I finally realized a change needed to be made if I ever wanted to be happy. I learned to love and appreciate Joy more when she was gone, because I loved her so much but couldn't be with her.

When I started drawing in prison I wasn't very good, but I thought I was good. When I decided to take art seriously, I practiced constantly. If I could see what it took to become good, I did what I needed to do to become better. Once I saw what it took to become good, why would I use techniques I now knew would produce bad work? This is simple to understand, yet life was the same way and for many years I never saw this. Once I could see and accept my personal faults, I had the ability to work on them.

When Joy left me, it broke me and I knew it was because I was bad. I loved this woman, yet I was hurting myself and it was hurting her to watch me waste my life away. She saw potential in me, even when I was blind to it. When she walked away this was my rock bottom and I started my journey to getting better. Many people had tried the tough love approach and it didn't work. However, to be ready to change, I needed to lose everything and really start looking within myself. I finally called myself on my own bullshit. When you spend a lifetime feeling like you're hot shit, it hurts to see the truth. I was finally starting to realize how I was insane, because I was doing the same things over and over again, but praying for better outcomes.

Prison does offer programs to help inmates, but a prisoner must want to make a change. I just finally got sick and tired of being sick and tired. I started to get involved in different programs, but I was still on the fence because I was afraid to let go of Dutch, the gangster/tough guy. I was a young misled kid who got in over his head and played a part that was fueled by my pride. Too much pride will get a young man killed.

Prison has a certain way of stunting certain men's growth because upon entering it seems like their mentality is frozen in time because they want to be who they were in the streets. This happens because these men want to hold onto the people they once were. The problem is, most inner-city men black or white, commit acts of violence in the early years of their lives when they are young, dumb and as the saying goes, full of cum. This is why you see a "Lord of the Fly's" mentality. The problems within prisons are started over juvenile things, the phone, TV or lack of respect. The phone and the TV are the department of corrections property and after we try to harm each other and are locked down, the next set of guys can pretend they own something.

Men in prison are big on respect, yet these same men didn't respect anything in their lives as free men. If one is to fall into these ideologies and ignorant patterns, how can they expect to change? I was one of these men. When I finally saw things for what they were I was angry. I was angry with myself for everything I had done. I always thought I was the clever one, yet I was the fool. Time and time again, I allowed myself to be used or did something to prove myself to people who didn't matter.

To truly grow as a person, one must be able to look at themselves and their faults. I have always been loyal to the men I was surrounded by but I wasn't loyal to the girls in my life or the people who wanted the best for me. It's hard to accept that men who didn't care about anything other than their personal gain, won my loyalty over those who cared. I was starting to understand emotions that I had locked away or numbed with drugs all my life. Understanding emotions was very difficult for me, but this is when I started to grow. It took me years of my life to figure out I just wanted to be loved. I had pushed a woman away who truly loved the good me. The me who was able to love and feel. The me who was able to love her.

My road has been rocky at times and Karma has visited me on several occasions. But I now believe I had to lose everything. I needed to question how I wanted the world to remember me and I needed to learn to have faith. I wish I could say I woke up one day and just figured it out, but this would be a lie. It took me far too long to grow up.

The love of my life has come back to me after 10 lonely years of not seeing the woman who first taught me how to love. The reality of her leaving was a lot to deal with, but I am so fortunate because I am in love with the most amazing woman who believes in me and my dreams. True love really has the ability to change anyone and anything.

I have many ideas about things that need to be changed with today's youth. I watch how inmates conduct themselves while they are a part of the "Scared Straight Program". The Scared Straight Program is a program for troubled youth, and the objective is to scare these kids and show them what a life of poor choices may lead to. I have seen inmates trying to scare these children by catcalling them like they're woman, or threatening them. I believe this approach needs work.

In my opinion, we should not scare these children, but show the harsh realities that may become their realities, if they continue taking the wrong path. Too often, kids are led in the wrong direction by influences who should know better. I believe the key is to identify troubled children and teach them about the consequences that come along with the choices they're making. It should not be done with fear but with realities they can identify with. I understand that children hang

241

in the street and join gangs because they're looking for a way to be accepted, because I was one of those children.

In America, we glorify the gangster. The problem is, we do not reveal the truth of what this life entails. Very few make it to become Tony Montana, and even Tony Montana was killed at the end of Scarface. The youth needs to understand, that real men, are the ones who raise their children and do their best to provide a better life for them. A better life than they had for themselves.

It sickens me that the cycle is repetitive when a father goes to prison and the son ends up following in his footsteps. I have seen far too many father and son duos in prison. I am just one man, but I believe it is my responsibility to do what I can to help make the change. I spent too many years promoting nonsense and I now feel compelled to balance the rest of my life with trying to help leave the world a better place. Upon my release, I would like to go to the inner cities and create programs where I will use art as my avenue to speak to children. I will do my best to teach them how they can be more than they believe they can be.

Fortunately, I am blessed because I have been able to mend fences with my family. Sadly, many inmates are not as fortunate. The sad reality is, society expects those who are not as fortunate upon their release from prison, to be assigned housing in shelters that are no better than prisons. Most men have not prepared themselves or came up with a way to do something different. Due to this, it is little wonder why they end up doing what they did to come to prison in the first place.

Upon my release, my dreams are much simpler than they were as a child. I look forward to being able to do the small things I had once taken for granted. I want to be able to walk hand and hand with my wife down a street, I look forward to being able to choose what I want to eat and most of all, I can't wait to wake up and see my sleeping angel next to me. In prison, I lost my enthusiasm for holidays because holidays in prison, mark the years and the missed opportunities to spend with family and friends. After so many years, you become numb to the fact you cannot be with your family on the days that mean the most to them. Because my wife is a Christmas nut, I now look forward to starting Christmas preparations by Halloween. This sounds crazy to me; however, this is the new type of crazy I look forward to.

When I came to prison in 1998, the internet was not a big deal and cell phones were only possessed by business men and drug dealers. Nowadays, it shocks me how seven and eight-year-old children have cell phones. I saw one of these contraptions at Grandma's funeral, and didn't even know where I was supposed to speak. Once upon a time, I really thought I knew it all. Now I must learn to deal with the fact that the average 8-year-old is smarter than me.

Life has a funny way of taking you on a journey you didn't plan. When I initially started writing this book, it was me preparing to leave my story behind. Yet my life has completely changed proving it is never too late to turn your life around. What once was considered the end of my story, is now my new beginning.

~The Beginning~

To Be Continued. . .

GALLERY

Jeff 3 Years Old

Jeff & Shane

Jeff 4 Years Old

Jeff 7 Years Old

Jeff Disney Trip 1991

Jeff Prison

Dread, Jeff & Misha

Jeff Prison

Mr. & Mrs. de Leyer

Jeff's Artwork

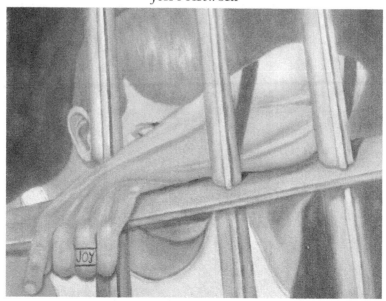

To view more of Jeff's Artwork please visit his website or follow him on Facebook & Instagram. For inquiries, please email info@jeffdeleyer.com

https://www.facebook.com/handgunstopaintbrushes
https://www.instagram.com/jeffdeleyer/
http://jeffdeleyer.com/

Made in the USA
Monee, IL
13 February 2022

91190501R00144